I0048534

The IT Consultant's Year of Intention

A Workbook Dedicated to Your Success

Karl W. Palachuk

The IT Consultant's Year of Intention

A Workbook Dedicated to Your Success

Karl W. Palachuk

Some pieces of this workbook were previously published in some form, or inspired by previous writings the author has published as blog posts at https://blog.smallbizthoughts.com and https://relaxfocussucceed.com/blog. All material is copyrighted by Karl W. Palachuk.

No animals were harmed in the making of this book, although there's a squirrel I better not find in my back yard again if he knows what's good for him.

ISBN Info: 978-1-942115-63-2 Paperback   978-1-942115-64-9 PDF   978-1-942115-65-6 Kindle/ebook

Published by

Great Little Book Publishing Co., Inc.

Sacramento, CA

GreatLittleBook.com / SmallBizThoughts.org

THE SMALL BIZ THOUGHTS TECHNOLOGY COMMUNITY

The IT Consultant's Year of Intention

Table of Contents

Quotes . . . to prime your reticular Activating System

"Life rewards action."

— Bill Black

"A budget tells us what we can't afford, but it doesn't keep us from buying it."

— William Feather

"A man's reach should exceed his grasp, or what's heaven for?"

— Robert Browning

Welcome to Next Year!

Preparing for a new year – with intention!

I am very pleased to present this workbook. I originally developed it for the members of my Small Biz Thoughts Technology Community (smallbizthoughts.org). It was well received – and members even used it for a class to prepare for the year ahead. So now I am making it available to consultants everywhere.

This workbook is intended to be used "This Year" to prepare for success "Next Year." Most business owners do this work in the final quarter of the year – if they do it at all! In some sense, it doesn't matter when you start planning for next year. I'm sure you've heard that the best day to start planning was yesterday. The next best day is today.

It's always good to finish off the business year with a little analysis. And then, you can dive into the next year with a plan for supreme success!

Note: We offer a class inside the Small Biz Thoughts Technology Community to go through this book. The class is held in November and December each year, but is also available on demand to Community members. The class is free inside the Community. For more information on the SBT Technology Community, see the final pages of this workbook.

Whether or not you join us in class, I hope you'll take some time to work through these exercises and prepare your business for a successful year. Each year has its own set of difficulties for the IT industry. But you know you'll do better *with* a plan than without a plan!

Using this Workbook

This workbook was created to help you clarify what success means to you . . . and to help you have an amazingly successful Next Year!

I know that sounds like a big promise. But here's the secret: It's all up to you. The more you put into it, the more you'll get out of it. As with so many things in life and business, you get to choose whether you will simply read through these exercises or stop, focus, and actually work through them.

Here are a few tips to help you get the most out of this workbook – and the New Year:

1. **Do not feel pressured to go through every exercise**. But please work through some of them! In some areas, you may feel like you've already "figured it out" and you don't need

to do any work. In other areas, you may be at a point in your career/life where you are ready to do some work.

2. **Use a pencil instead of a pen**. This is really a way of saying be flexible! Take lots of notes, but consider everything a "work in progress." Even if you make a really big, important decision, write it down in pencil. You can always highlight it, write over it in permanent marker, and even make a poster with your decision. But keep the mindset that every decision you make can be reversed. With luck, you'll keep working ON your business for the rest of your career.

3. **Pick up this workbook at least once per month**. No pressure. Remember, you can always start over whenever you want. It's your business!

4. **Be action-focused!** That means that these exercises should be more than merely mental exercises. At the end of the day (at the end of the year), the only actions that matter are those that you actually execute. While thinking about your business is good, making changes that move you forward is what really matters.

5. **Set goals and track them**. And don't worry. You can always change your goals. This isn't a game, and it's not intended to be "just another thing" you add to your to-do list. Ideally, you'll use this workbook to get yourself into the habit of spending time working ON your business.

We have to admit right off that we cannot control the world in which we operate our business. Nothing proves that better than the year 2020. But remember: Every year is crazy and unpredictable. Some are stranger than others. But there really never is a true "normal."

There's a great quote from Field Marshal Helmuth Karl Bernhard Graf von Moltke:

"No plan survives first contact with the enemy."

Perhaps a better way of saying this is the immortal words of boxer Mike Tyson: **"Everyone has a plan until they get punched in the mouth."**

The global pandemic was a punch in the mouth. Inflation's a punch in the mouth. Recessions are a punch in the mouth. Manufacturers cancelling your most profitable products are a punch in the mouth. As the old cliché goes: It's always something.

Whatever you had planned for in January is guaranteed to be different from the year that followed. That's true every year, especially in technology. Our world spins a bit faster than the rest of the world.

The wisdom behind the quotes above is:

> 1) You have to have a plan.

> 2) But you better be flexible, because the plan may not last long.

Remember: You've got a community to help you out! Join us online. Talk about your challenges and ideas. You can even build your own groups of members who are facing similar challenges or taking on similar opportunities.

Begin with The End in Mind

If you work "on" your success regularly, you're used to zooming in and out on your goals. For example, you focus for a long time on sales. You make some decisions, put some things in motion, and then focus on something else. At some point, you have a "big picture" discussion that includes your sales strategy. And then, after a time, you focus very closely on sales again.

We do this all the time in our business. You can't do two things at once (really). You can only time-slice, like a computer. You can work on one thing for a while, then switch to something else. Sales, service, employees, finances, customer service, a temporary crisis, marketing, product evaluation, etc. The list goes on and on.

This workbook is intended to give you some "starter" tools for working on various pieces of your business from various angles. I have an essay at the beginning of the workbook that I *really* want you to read first. I know that people like to jump right into the work part of a workbook, but I encourage you to "prime your brain" first.

That essay will help you understand how workbooks like this actually help you focus your attention and drive greater success in your business. So, please plan to read it as you begin your work. Warning: If you read it last, you may curse me and then begin working through this entire workbook again.

The big-big goal of this workbook is to help you kick-start the new year and get it headed in the right direction. I want you to spend some time thinking about what you'll do in March and April and May of next year. I want you to set some goals about employees, finances, and product offerings.

With a tip of the hat to Michael Gerber, I want you to work ON your business, not just IN your business. Don't fumble through your year. Start with intention and create the year you want to have.

Last Year, This Year, and Next Year

Throughout this book I will use three phrases that I hope are very clear:

- Last Year
- This Year
- Next Year

This Year simply refers to the year we are in right now. For example, let's say you are going through these exercises in the Fall of 2025. "This Year" is 2025.

So, naturally, Next Year represents the year you are planning for. From there, we might discuss the next three years or the next five years. I will try to be clear and not confusing. Just remember to use *This Year* as the anchor. Finally, Last Year is simply the year before this year. We don't use this a great deal, but we do from time to time.

Note on forms: I have printed a few of each form in this workbook, if you choose to use them or photocopy them. Additional forms are available in the downloads in PDF format. You may print copies as you need.

Your Downloadable Content

This book includes a few additional downloads what you will find very helpful. These include the forms in PDF format plus a few other goodies.

If you purchased this book from Small Biz Thoughts, you should have received a download link when your purchase was completed. If you accessed it in the Small Biz Thoughts Technology Community, the downloads accompany the book.

If you purchased from Amazon, Barnes and Noble, or another reseller, you can register at **store.smallbizthoughts.com**. Please have your purchase receipt ready to register. You'll need the Order ID. If your purchase somewhere else, you'll need to forward proof of purchase to us.

Your feedback is always welcome. Questions about downloads? Email concierge@smallbizthoughts.com.

Quotes . . . to prime your reticular Activating System

"Always Treat Your Employees Exactly As You Want Them To Treat Your Best Customers."

— Stephen Covey

"Big people are always giving someone credit and taking blame; little people are always seeking credit and giving blame."

— Charlie "Tremendous" Jones

"Constant Fine-Tuning is the true path to wisdom, so learn a little every day."

— Jack Canfield, Mark Victor Hansen, and Les Hewitt

Priming Your Brain

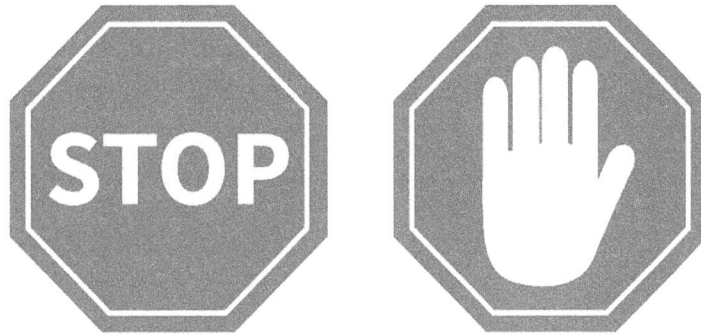

STOP

Seriously.

Please do yourself a big favor. Before you dig into the rest of this workbook, please grab a pen (or pencil) and answer these questions. You can just jot down some thoughts. Keywords. Bullet points. Whatever makes you happy.

Whether you write your answers in this book or on a piece of paper, I highly encourage you write by hand on some kind of paper and not type on a computer, phone, or other device. The tactile nature of writing your thoughts will help to make them higher priority in your mind.

Note: We'll come back to these questions a bit after the first exercise.

Ready? Good. Here are the questions:

1. How has your business been going so far this year?

_____

_____

_____

2. Is there anything that troubles you about your business now or in the months ahead? If so, what?

_____

_____

_____

3. Who are your favorite clients?

_____

_____

_____

4. Do you have the talent (your own or your employees) you need to be successful in the year ahead?

_____

_____

_____

5. What do you like MOST about your business? Do you get enough of it?

_____

_____

_____

Priming Your Brain – An Essay by Karl W. Palachuk

(A quick intro to the reticular activating system.)

I love learning about the human brain. Being human is a pretty amazing thing. People go on and on about how smart dolphins are. But there have been zero hospitals or space ships built by dolphins.

I digress.

Some say that our self-awareness is one of the defining factors of humans. We can learn about our bodies and use that knowledge to improve ourselves. That is more true regarding the brain than anything else.

Aside from being an efficient chemical factory for producing hormones that affect happiness, pleasure, body control, and mood, the brain is a masterful collection of information systems and sub-systems. One of my favorite sub-systems is called the **reticular activating system**. The reticular formation is a set of interconnected nuclei that are located throughout the brain stem. The ascending reticular activating system (RAS) represents a series of connections made between the brain stem and the higher parts of the brain.

The RAS is a miraculous system for controlling habits and perceptions in humans. On one hand, it affects the way you see the world, filtering millions of stimuli into a few things you pay attention to. On the other hand, it reinforces behavior and beliefs. So, for example, we tend to filter out information that doesn't fit our current beliefs. (This should help explain a great deal of the political discussion on Facebook.)

Here's the coolest part as far as I'm concerned: the RAS does a lot of work automatically (controlling automated functions of the body, filtering information, helping you sleep, etc .), but it can also be *manipulated by your intentions*. And when that happens, your intentions can become magnified very powerfully. Here's what I mean.

Everyone's had the experience of buying a car and then seeing that car all over town. Those cars were always driving all over town: You just didn't notice them because you didn't care. You have to filter out virtually everything you're exposed to or you would not be able to function. The RAS does that filtering. At the same time, you can choose to focus on specific things. You can tune into the color blue, or BMWs, or plastic ducks. Most of the time, these "choices" are unconscious. They just happen. But you can make conscious choices to focus on specific information.

Let's try an example. You may have heard of the concept of blockchain. Blockchain is a cool new technology for creating secure transactions. It's being used more and more all the time. Many companies are investing in blockchain. Say the words out loud: *blockchain*.

There. I've told you almost nothing about blockchain. But I've planted the seed in your consciousness. You've probably heard the phrase blockchain before, but you have not paid attention to it unless there's a reason to. Now, I've dragged it out of the background fog and into the forefront of your attention. Watch over the next 1-2 days and you will probably see or hear the phrase blockchain. This phrase has been floating around, just outside your consciousness. Now it will become more visible for a short time.

"Short time" is key here. If you have no reason to pay attention to blockchain, this raised consciousness will fade quickly – precisely because it has no value in your life.

Now consider something else. Perhaps you want to grow your business, lose weight, learn a new skill, get your garden into shape, or any other goal. If you take time to bring that goal into your conscious brain, the RAS will recognize that it has value for you . . . and begin focusing on it more and more. The RAS becomes an amplifier for your goals.

On more than one occasion, I've had a "great" business idea that flashed into my head. I took time to sit down, write out notes, make some drawings, and maybe even do some financial calculations. In other words, I focused very heavily on this idea for an hour or so. And guess what? All day the next day, it seemed that every conversation helped promote that idea. People popped into my head that might be able to help me. The radio had a story about something on a related topic. And so forth.

> The point is: Once I chose to give an idea a certain amount of attention, the RAS helped me give it more and more attention.

Now, if you practice this regularly, your RAS will help you amplify your focus. But only for a short period of time . . . until you continually choose to focus more. If you keep focusing on the subject again and again, your RAS will renew its attention more and more. It's a lot like cramming your way through on online course. You can ignore it for a while and your brain will have no reason to put attention on it. But when you buckle down and study every day, your brain redoubles your efforts . . . and begins working on the problem in the background when you are not even aware that your brain is working on your behalf.

All success comes back to the concept of focus. In my book *Relax Focus Succeed*, I say that you get better at whatever you put your attention on. Other people have said things like, "Whatever you put your attention on expands." That's absolutely true. You can spend your days responding to the random stimuli of the universe, or you can choose to focus your attention – And your good friend the reticular activating system helps you focus even more.

Two Filters – Hacking Your RAS

The RAS provides two types of filters. First, it keeps *out* millions of things we don't need to pay attention to. After all, we're exposed to literally millions of impressions per day. Second, it helps to focus more clearly on what *is* important.

That second part is the most interesting to me because we can "hack" our RAS to help us focus even more. Because the RAS helps us decide what is important, we can feed it stimuli. Your conscious brain can literally seed what your unconscious brain pays attention to.

All of the exercises in this workbook are opportunities for you to hack your RAS. Every time you think about your finances, you move it up a bit in your brain's priority system. The same is true with service delivery, customer service, sales, marketing, vendor management, and all the other details of running your business.

This is exactly why you need to <u>execute</u> these exercises – don't just read through them and ignore them!

In *Relax Focus Succeed*, I give an analogy between the brain and a filing system. All day long, you go through your day pulling cards out of the filing system and throwing them on the floor. Some cards are problems, some are experiences, some are ideas. And then, at night, your unconscious brain picks up the cards, sorts them, and files them away again. Every once in a while, it picks up a "problem" card and an "idea" card that match. Your unconscious brain has solved a problem!

But you're asleep and you're not aware that you've solved a problem. That's where meditation comes in. Meditation allows your brain to relax and do that background work while you're still awake. Of course, it's all much more complicated than that. But here's how you can use meditation to seed your RAS so that your focus is pointed directly where you want it.

You've heard of "mindfulness" meditation. Many people define this as a type of meditation where you try to clear your mind of all thoughts. For example, you just sit there and, when a thought wanders into your mind, you acknowledge it and then set it aside. Other people define mindfulness as simply experiencing what's going on. In this variant, you sit there and name the things that enter your attention. A truck driving past. A bird. The breeze. Someone walking.

In both variants of mindfulness, you are attempting to NOT think – to not solve problems, not worry about money, not plan the day ahead, etc. It seems miraculous, but this lack of focusing on anything often results in major epiphanies. We've all had the experience of coming up with a great idea while you're in the shower. That's because it's just you and your brain with no outside stimuli from radio, TV, the Internet, etc.

Let me suggest a technique that I use. I think you'll be amazed at how easy it is.

First, choose an object for focus. It might be a poem, an idea for work, a problem with the kids, etc. Anything. Sit quietly and think about the object of focus. If you wish, take notes. The overall idea is to simply fill your mind – your attention – with thoughts and questions about this topic. I generally take anywhere from five to thirty minutes for this. The more time you give it, the more focused you become.

Here's what's going on physiologically: You are telling your RAS in no uncertain terms that you have something that needs your focus. You are doing this in a relaxed manner without frenzy or panic. You are, in fact, simply setting its agenda and letting it know that this is important to you.

Second, put an end to that and move into mindfulness meditation. Find a technique that works for you. STOP thinking about the problem you just spent time on. Focus on your breathing. Or do a whole-body scan. For beginnings, I think full body scans or Yoga Nidra (Google it) are excellent. Take as much time as you can. I recommend no less than fifteen minutes. If you can do thirty, that's even better.

There's no cheating here. You really are trying to clear your mind of everything. Clean the slate. Relax. Be open. Just experience your breath moving in and out. When ideas float by, acknowledge them and then move your attention back to your breath.

Third, go about your day. That's it. Just do whatever you need to do. Go to work. Cook dinner. Have a beer. Enjoy some television. Whatever you do, just do that.

Here's what's really going on: You have put serious, focused attention on an object (problem, idea, etc.). That has given your RAS notice that you want attention on this. And as you go through your day, you will notice that lots of things seem to be related to the object of your focus. People you meet have ideas that are related. Snippets of news you see on the Internet are related to it. Comments you overhear are related.

It's as if the world has conspired to help you achieve your goals, solve your problems, help you find funding for a project, or whatever you need. In reality, you have simply applied a filter. You are paying less attention to little, unimportant things, and more attention to the one thing you identified as needing your attention.

Imagine if you do this every day. Figure out what is the most important thing that needs your attention. And then spend the day finding that thing everywhere you look.

Way back in my college days, I was a camp counselor for the YMCA. Session after session, I had a cabin full of seven-year-olds. One of my favorite distractions was to give them a basic assignment such as:

- ❖ Everyone go out and bring back a red leaf
- ❖ Everyone go out and find a stick with a "Y"
- ❖ Everyone go out and bring me a small, smooth rock

These were simple assignments and everyone was always successful. This exercise with your RAS is basically the same thing. You're telling your unconscious attention span to go focus on a specific object . . . and it does just that. – "Go find me a solution to this problem."

The best part about priming your attention span is that it just works. The simple fact that you put your attention on something creates the focus that stays on that thing all day.

Try it! Make it a regular part of your success in the year ahead – and all the other years ahead!

About Those Questions

So, why did I make a big deal of asking you those questions before reading this essay? You guessed it – to prime your RAS and get you thinking about your business. Challenges, clients, and so forth.

You have many kinds of information in your brain. Some is important, some is not. Some is related to business, most is not. So, with a few questions, I hope to start priming your brain to enter the "business analysis" mode as you go through this workbook.

It doesn't take much. You don't need to spend an hour looking at your financial reports to be able to be in the groove of thinking about your financials. Perhaps one good question will do the trick.

Here's how we'll integrate "Prime Questions" into this workbook. At the beginning of each chapter, I literally call out a few Prime Questions. I promise you will get more out of this entire workbook if you grab a pen or pencil and write out some thoughts about the Prime Questions for each chapter.

I have repeated all of these Prime Questions at the end of the workbook. Plus, there's space for you to think of your own. If you come up with really good questions that prime your brain, please send them to me. If you give me permission, I might even use them in future versions of this workbook.

Now, let's dig in and start thinking about YOUR business and the year ahead.

Quotes . . . to prime your reticular Activating System

"Courtesy is the shortest distance between two people."

— Anonymous

"Doing what you are good at will only make you good; focusing on what you can potentially do better than any other organization is the only path to greatness."

— Jim Collins

"Don't screw around. Start now. Find an excuse. Do something. Do anything. Get going. Posthaste."

— Tom Peters

Small Biz Thoughts Technology Community

Report on This Year

Prime Questions

1. Did you start this year with a budget and a plan? If so, how are you doing?

_____

_____

2. What's the biggest challenge you have today, and looking through the end of the year?

_____

_____

3. How much do you like your current mix of productions and services, given current pricing?

_____

_____

There are two primary pieces to your summary of this year, so far. First, there's a quick evaluation of the goals you set, and your progress toward those goals. Second, there's the financial look at your business. I _highly_ encourage you to do both parts. Don't just look at the money and think that somehow represents what's going on in your company.

Part One: Report on Goals from the Current Year

All of these items are discussed in some detail in the next section. But as an overview, you should be able to make enough notes here to get a sense of how the year has gone so far.

Notes on Company Mission, Vision, and Values. _____

_____

_____

_____

Big-Big-Big Goals. What are the long-term (multi-year) goals you had in mind when you set out your Annual Goals for This Year? _____

_____

_____

_____

Annual Goals – for The Year. These are your big-picture goals for this year. With luck, you had at least three major goals for the year.

Goal #1 for the year: _____

_____

_____

Progress made toward goal: _____

_____

_____

_____

Notes for Next Year regarding this goal: _____

_____

_____

_____

Goal #2 for the year: _____

_____

_____

_____

Progress made toward goal: _____

_____

_____

_____

Notes for Next Year regarding this goal: _____

_____

_____

_____

Annual Goals – This Year. These are your big-picture goals for the current year. With luck, you had at least three major goals for the year.

Goal #1 for this year: _____

_____

_____

_____

Progress made toward goal: _____

_____

_____

_____

Notes for Next Year regarding this goal: _____

_____

_____

Goal #2 for this year: _____

_____

_____

_____

Progress made toward goal: _____

_____

_____

_____

Notes for Next Year regarding this goal: _____

_____

_____

Goal #3 for this year: _____

_____

_____

_____

Progress made toward goal: _____

_____

_____

_____

Notes for Next Year regarding this goal: _____

_____

_____

Goal #4 for this year: _____

_____

_____

_____

Progress made toward goal: _____

_____

_____

_____

Notes for Next Year regarding this goal: _____

_____

_____

Part Two: Money Stuff for This Year

For the money side of things, you need to spend some time with your finance tool (QuickBooks, Xero, Sage, etc.) and your bookkeeper. The goal here is not to lay out your entire chart of accounts. We are looking for a high-level overview.

Ideally, you have information for last year, the current year, plus a projection for next year. Note: you cannot simply project a ten percent increase across the board. You need some reason for whatever numbers you put into your projections.

Remember: You might change your plans. But you should at least start with a plan!

On the next page, fill in information from the financial report you have from last year and this year. You will probably need to combine some categories in order to generate all these numbers. I have attempted to highlight the "big" numbers like labor and combine smaller numbers. If you're going to make changes in your spending habits, you're most likely going to focus on the larger numbers.

Of course, this simplified "budget" is in an Excel download file. Feel free to add additional detail and customize as needed. The more realistically it reflects your business, the better.

See next page.

Money Stuff - Budget

Category	Last year:	This Year	Next Year
Revenue			
Hardware/Software	$	$	$
Recurring Revenue	$	$	$
Hourly Labor	$	$	$
Other	$	$	$
Total Revenue	**$**	**$**	**$**
Expenses			
Cost of Goods Sold			
- Hardware/Software	$	$	$
- Recurring Revenue	$	$	$
- Hourly Labor	$	$	$
- Other	$	$	$
Advertising	$	$	$
Employee Benefits	$	$	$
Insurance	$	$	$
Marketing	$	$	$
Office Expenses	$	$	$
Payroll (Labor)	$	$	$
Payroll Taxes	$	$	$
Rent	$	$	$
Taxes	$	$	$
Utilities	$	$	$
Total Expenses	**$**	**$**	**$**
Total Profit (Loss)	**$**	**$**	**$**

Notes on your budget: _____

_____

_____

_____

_____

_____

_____

_____

_____

_____

_____

_____

_____

_____

_____

_____

_____

_____

_____

_____

_____

_____

_____

_____

_____

_____

Company Goals for Next Year

Prime Questions

1. Are you looking forward to next year with hope, concern, or some mixture of these? Why so?

_____

_____

2. Are you planning any big changes in your business for next year? (This might be with regard to clients, your service offering, employees, or whatever else.)

_____

_____

3. In the big-big picture, will your business be essentially the same next your, or will something important change?

_____

_____

As you plan for the new year, you should write down your goals. Put dates or deadlines on them, and determine how you will measure success. And remember: Just because you wrote it down doesn't mean you can't change it! These are your goals. You should write them down. But you should also evaluate them periodically.

This workbook doesn't have room to go into a huge goal-setting exercise. Instead, I'll try to give you some framework. Take what works and adjust it for your company, your structure, and your personal habits.

Here's the basic structure:

Mission, Vision, and Values. This is beyond the scope of this workbook, but if you've worked through these things (and you should), write them down here. It doesn't have to be anything big or fancy. Any guidance is good.

Big-Big-Big Goals. These are goals so big that they don't fit in one year. For example, getting to a big revenue goal, selling the company, becoming the largest MSP in the state. You might reach these goals in the year ahead, but it's more likely that you'll reach them in three to five years. This is important to write down, because you can then see where next year fits in the big (big-big-big) picture.

Annual Goals for Next Year. These are the big-picture goals for next year. What will revenue look like? How many new clients will you sign? What will your staff look like? Will you acquire a building, lease a car, or revamp your cybersecurity offering? Write it down here.

Quarterly Goals. These are more manageable chunks. They contribute to your annual goals, of course, but also need separate measures.

Goal Tracking Overview

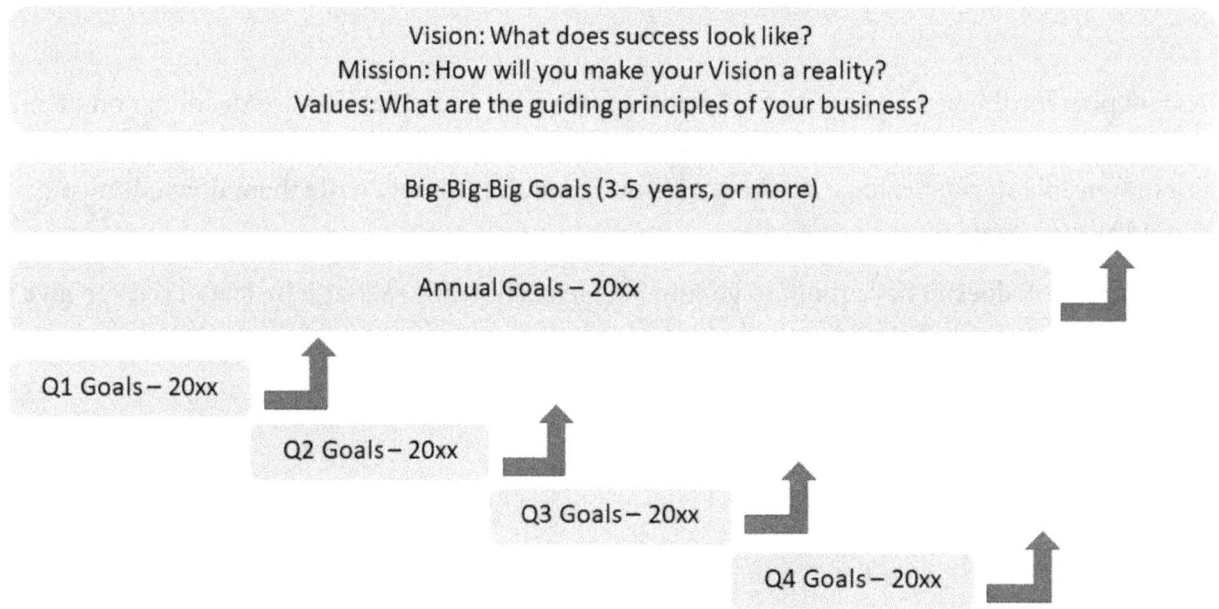

Vision: What does success look like?
Mission: How will you make your Vision a reality?
Values: What are the guiding principles of your business?

Big-Big-Big Goals (3-5 years, or more)

Annual Goals – 20xx

Q1 Goals – 20xx

Q2 Goals – 20xx

Q3 Goals – 20xx

Q4 Goals – 20xx

On the worksheets, I've provided a space for you to note how each set of goals fits in the bigger picture goals. This is helpful as you set goals for various departments and team members, as well as yourself.

The Basics:

Company Vision Statement: What does success look like? _____

_____

_____

_____

Company Mission Statement: How will you make your vision come true? _____

_____

_____

_____

Company Values: _____

_____

_____

_____

_____

_____

Quotes . . . to prime your reticular Activating System

Failure to hit the bull's-eye is never the fault of the target. To improve your aim improve yourself.

— Gilbert Arland

"Have patience. All things are difficult before they become easy."

— Sa'di

"I am a great believer in Luck. The harder I work the more of it I seem to have."

— Coleman Cox

Company Goals for Next Year

The Big-Big-Big Goals

These are longer-term goals that guide our company going forward. All of next year's goals exist to push toward the successful achievement of these longer-term goals.

Goal: _____

_____

Target date: _____

_____

This advances our company vision/mission by: _____

_____

Progress toward this goal is measured by: _____

_____

Notes: _____

_____

Goal: _____

_____

Target date: _____

_____

This advances our company vision/mission by: _____

_____

Progress toward this goal is measured by: _____

_____

Notes: _____

_____

Company Goals for Next Year – Continued

The Big-Big-Big Goals

Goal: _____

_____

Target date: _____

_____

This advances our company vision/mission by: _____

_____

Progress toward this goal is measured by: _____

_____

Notes: _____

_____

Goal: _____

_____

Target date: _____

_____

This advances our company vision/mission by: _____

_____

Progress toward this goal is measured by: _____

_____

Notes: _____

_____

Company Goals for Next Year – Continued

Annual Goals for Next Year

Goal: _____

_____

This advances our long-term company goals by: _____

_____

Progress toward this goal is measured by: _____

_____

Department Actions in Support of this Goal

Administration/Front Office: _____

_____

Service Department: _____

_____

Sales Department: _____

_____

Customer Service Department: _____

_____

Primary actions we are taking in support of this goal: _____

_____

Visible measures of success are: _____

_____

Notes: _____

_____

Company Goals for Next Year– Continued

Annual Goals for Next Year

Goal: _____

_____

This advances our long-term company goals by: _____

_____

Progress toward this goal is measured by: _____

_____

Department Actions in Support of this Goal

Administration/Front Office: _____

_____

Service Department: _____

_____

Sales Department: _____

_____

Customer Service Department: _____

_____

Primary actions we are taking in support of this goal: _____

_____

Visible measures of success are: _____

_____

Notes: _____

_____

Company Goals for Next Year– Continued

Annual Goals for Next Year

Goal: _____

_____

This advances our long-term company goals by: _____

_____

Progress toward this goal is measured by: _____

_____

Department Actions in Support of this Goal

Administration/Front Office: _____

_____

Service Department: _____

_____

Sales Department: _____

_____

Customer Service Department: _____

_____

Primary actions we are taking in support of this goal: _____

_____

Visible measures of success are: _____

_____

Notes: _____

_____

Quotes . . . to prime your reticular Activating System

If you don't know what you want to do, it's harder to do it.

— Malcolm Forbes

"If you don't like where you are, change it! You're not a tree."

— Jim Rohn

"If you find a path with no obstacles, it probably doesn't lead anywhere."

— Frank A. Clark

Company Goals for Next Year– Continued

Quarterly Goals – Q1 Next Year

Goal: _____

_____

This advances our annual company goals by: _____

_____

Progress toward this goal is measured by: _____

_____

Department Actions in Support of this Goal

Administration/Front Office: _____

_____

Service Department: _____

_____

Sales Department: _____

_____

Customer Service Department: _____

_____

Primary actions we are taking in support of this goal: _____

_____

Visible measures of success are: _____

_____

Notes: _____

_____

Company Goals for Next Year– Continued

Quarterly Goals – Q1 Next Year

Goal: _____

_____

This advances our annual company goals by: _____

_____

Progress toward this goal is measured by: _____

_____

Department Actions in Support of this Goal

Administration/Front Office: _____

_____

Service Department: _____

_____

Sales Department: _____

_____

Customer Service Department: _____

_____

Primary actions we are taking in support of this goal: _____

_____

Visible measures of success are: _____

_____

Company Goals for Next Year– Continued

Quarterly Goals – Q1 Next Year

Goal: _____

_____

This advances our annual company goals by: _____

_____

Progress toward this goal is measured by: _____

_____

Department Actions in Support of this Goal

Administration/Front Office: _____

_____

Service Department: _____

_____

Sales Department: _____

_____

Customer Service Department: _____

_____

Primary actions we are taking in support of this goal: _____

_____

Visible measures of success are: _____

_____

Company Goals for Next Year– Continued

Quarterly Goals – Q2 Next Year

Goal: _____

_____

This advances our annual company goals by: _____

_____

Progress toward this goal is measured by: _____

_____

Department Actions in Support of this Goal

Administration/Front Office: _____

_____

Service Department: _____

_____

Sales Department: _____

_____

Customer Service Department: _____

_____

Primary actions we are taking in support of this goal: _____

_____

Visible measures of success are: _____

_____

Company Goals for Next Year– Continued

Quarterly Goals – Q2 Next Year

Goal: _____

_____

This advances our annual company goals by: _____

_____

Progress toward this goal is measured by: _____

_____

Department Actions in Support of this Goal

Administration/Front Office: _____

_____

Service Department: _____

_____

Sales Department: _____

_____

Customer Service Department: _____

_____

Primary actions we are taking in support of this goal: _____

_____

Visible measures of success are: _____

_____

Company Goals for Next Year– Continued

Quarterly Goals – Q2 Next Year

Goal: _____

_____

This advances our annual company goals by: _____

_____

Progress toward this goal is measured by: _____

_____

Department Actions in Support of this Goal

Administration/Front Office: _____

_____

Service Department: _____

_____

Sales Department: _____

_____

Customer Service Department: _____

_____

Primary actions we are taking in support of this goal: _____

_____

Visible measures of success are: _____

_____

Quotes . . . to prime your reticular Activating System

"It is not given to me to know how many steps are necessary in order to reach my goal. . . . Always will I take another step."

— Og Mandino

"It is often easier to fight for a principle than to live up to it."

— Adlai Stevenson

"It's not that I'm smarter. It's just that I stay with problems longer."

— Albert Einstein

Small Biz Thoughts Technology Community

Company Goals for Next Year– Continued

Quarterly Goals – Q3 Next Year

Goal: _____

_____

This advances our annual company goals by: _____

_____

Progress toward this goal is measured by: _____

_____

Department Actions in Support of this Goal

Administration/Front Office: _____

_____

Service Department: _____

_____

Sales Department: _____

_____

Customer Service Department: _____

_____

Primary actions we are taking in support of this goal: _____

_____

Visible measures of success are: _____

_____

Company Goals for Next Year– Continued

Quarterly Goals – Q3 Next Year

Goal: _____

_____

This advances our annual company goals by: _____

_____

Progress toward this goal is measured by: _____

_____

Department Actions in Support of this Goal

Administration/Front Office: _____

_____

Service Department: _____

_____

Sales Department: _____

_____

Customer Service Department: _____

_____

Primary actions we are taking in support of this goal: _____

_____

Visible measures of success are: _____

_____

Company Goals for Next Year– Continued

Quarterly Goals – Q3 Next Year

Goal: _____

_____

This advances our annual company goals by: _____

_____

Progress toward this goal is measured by: _____

_____

Department Actions in Support of this Goal

Administration/Front Office: _____

_____

Service Department: _____

_____

Sales Department: _____

_____

Customer Service Department: _____

_____

Primary actions we are taking in support of this goal: _____

_____

Visible measures of success are: _____

_____

Company Goals for Next Year– Continued

Quarterly Goals – Q4 Next Year

Goal: _____

_____

This advances our annual company goals by: _____

_____

Progress toward this goal is measured by: _____

_____

Department Actions in Support of this Goal

Administration/Front Office: _____

_____

Service Department: _____

_____

Sales Department: _____

_____

Customer Service Department: _____

_____

Primary actions we are taking in support of this goal: _____

_____

Visible measures of success are: _____

_____

Company Goals for Next Year– Continued

Quarterly Goals – Q4 Next Year

Goal: _____

_____

This advances our annual company goals by: _____

_____

Progress toward this goal is measured by: _____

_____

Department Actions in Support of this Goal

Administration/Front Office: _____

_____

Service Department: _____

_____

Sales Department: _____

_____

Customer Service Department: _____

_____

Primary actions we are taking in support of this goal: _____

_____

Visible measures of success are: _____

_____

Company Goals for Next Year– Continued

Quarterly Goals – Q4 Next Year

Goal: _____

_____

This advances our annual company goals by: _____

_____

Progress toward this goal is measured by: _____

_____

Department Actions in Support of this Goal

Administration/Front Office: _____

_____

Service Department: _____

_____

Sales Department: _____

_____

Customer Service Department: _____

_____

Primary actions we are taking in support of this goal: _____

_____

Visible measures of success are: _____

_____

Quotes . . . to prime your reticular Activating System

"It's not your commitment I'm worried about. . . . It's your commitment to your commitment."

— Kenneth Blanchard and Robert Lorber

"Keep your eyes on the stars and your feet on the ground."

— Theodore Roosevelt

Laboring toward distant aims sets the mind in a higher key and puts us at our best.

— Charles Henry Parkhurst

Conference Goals Next Year

Prime Questions

1. When you attend conferences, where do you find the most value? (e.g., networking, meeting vendors, travel)

_____

_____

2. Which kind of conferences do you get the most value from?

_____

_____

3. After a conference, what do you do to "process" what you learned and the contacts you made?

_____

_____

Conferences, workshops, and seminars are a great way to stay up to date on developments within your chosen profession. They're also a great way to learn new technologies, find out about new vendors, and to meet partners from around the country and the world.

While I encourage you to attend these events, I also caution you against attending too many. At some point, you've heard all the presentations and met all the vendors. You also need to spend time processing this information and putting it to work in your business.

Unless you have specific reasons to do otherwise, I encourage you to attend one or two "national" conferences and one or two regional conferences per year. If you add a few vendor-specific roadshows or workshops, you'll be at about half a dozen events per year. Ideally, you will not need to travel for most them.

This workbook contains a few worksheets for taking advantage of conferences. But, if you attend more, you can always photocopy a page and keep track of more.

These forms are intended to help you take notes and attend these conferences with intention. That is, you'll start with a clear understanding of *why* you're attending each event, and what you hope to achieve. It's also helpful to evaluate each event. Was it valuable enough to take a day out of the office?

Remember, you need to spend time working *on* your business – but don't fool yourself and pretend you're working on your business when the event turns out to be a waste of time.

When I say to attend with intention, I simply mean that you should have some goals in mind. Who do you want to meet? Which new products do you want to learn about? Which speakers do you want to see? And so forth.

If attending a seminar results in **no change of behavior** inside your company, then it has little or no value. As with everything else, you need to consume knowledge, then put it into action. If you constantly consume new information but don't do anything useful with it, you are better off using that time for something else.

Summary recommendations:

1) Have a reason for attending the conference. Write it down.

2) Attend – really attend the conference. Pay attention. Ask questions. Participate. Do not sit in the back of the room reading email and closing service tickets. Take notes.

3) Evaluate the conference when it's over. What actions will you take as a result? Which web sites will you visit? Who will you email? Will you test-drive a product or service?

Conferences and workshops generally take at least a whole day. If you need to travel, they tend to take more than a day. In addition to the cost of the event, you have airfare or other travel expenses, plus hotel. It can easily cost $500-1,000 to attend an event. Make sure you get that value from attending!

Many years ago, when I first started paying to attend events, I developed a habit of tracking when and whether the event paid for itself. For example, if I paid $249 for a one-day seminar, I would take notes and evaluate the information. At some point, one of three things would happen. Ideally, I would hear a great *nugget* of information and say to myself, "That information will make or save me the price of this seminar."

Another alternative is that I would evaluate the event when it was over, and determine that enough smaller pieces of information had made it worth the price of admission. I can honestly say that I rarely attended a paid seminar that did not pay for itself. Some were worth one hundred; some one thousand; and a few worth more than that.

Ironically, the only event that really stands out as not paying for itself was a $7,000 three-day seminar from one of my true mentors. The only thing I learned was that I had learned everything I could from that mentor. Shortly after that, I started charging that organization whenever they asked me to speak. So it all worked out in the long run.

Here's the point: People who build information-based services – like seminars and conferences – work really hard to make sure you get your money's worth. In fact, there's an informal code in the events business: Provide ten times as much value as the attendee expects. As a rule, I've found that to be true for all events that cost at least $199.

Remember: You get out of it what you put into it.

Commit to improving yourself and your business. Conferences and workshops can play a big role in that. But it means you need to go in with a learning mindset – and come out with a list of actions that you'll implement in your personal life or in your business.

What to Do After the Conference

Note: After the *Conference Notes* and *Conference Evaluation* sections, there's a *Conference Follow-Up Checklist*.

In addition to simply attending a conference or seminar, you should execute an intention "debriefing" with yourself about the event experience. After all, if you've set goals and evaluated the event, you should have some follow-up to do.

I'm sure you've heard the advice, "Start with the end in mind." That certainly applies with conferences. You need to decide what your goals are before you get to the conference. You'll write this into the *Conference Notes* form below.

A few possibilities are:

- Technical education
- Business education
- Meet people or network
- Engage with a vendor
- Find new technologies I might want to integrate into my business
- Learn how other people are addressing my current challenges
- Personal growth
- Try to find an answer to a very specific problem
- Get free swag for the kids

Once you know why you're going to the conference, you can create a plan of action for the conference, and you can evaluate whether it was worthwhile.

So, first, you need to define why you're attending the event. Second, you need to execute your attendance based on that. If, for example, you are looking to meet people and network, then go do that. If you're looking for a new RMM tool, then you'll want to hit the vendor booths and talk to attendees about their experience.

In other words, do NOT hang out with your friends the whole time. Mingle, meet people, collect business cards, and take notes. For all the info on business cards and what to do with them, see the section below dedicated to business cards.

I tend to write notes on the backs of business cards. I also keep 3x5 cards and post-it notes with me. I travel with an envelope and stuff all those things into the envelope, along with receipts from the trip. That way, when I get home, that envelope contains everything I need to "do" or take care of after the conference.

After the Conference . . .

Okay, so you've planned for the conference and you've executed your plan. Now you're going to head home with three things that need further action:

1. People (connections)

2. Products and Services

3. Ideas and Action Steps

Make sure you have a process for scanning business cards. Personally, I encourage you to literally hand this off to an administrative assistant. They can scan the cards right into your Outlook, your CRM, Constant Contact, or whatever you use to organize contacts.

Have your admin set aside any cards with hand-written notes on them (after scanning). Sometimes, the request is easy (e.g., send a meeting request). Your admin should be able to take care of these. Other notes might be more complicated. You should take the cards back – but be sure to follow up as promised!

Once cards are scanned and promises are kept, throw the cards in the recycle bin. Old bundles of cards with rubber bands around, rattling around in the bottom of a desk drawer, are useless.

See the follow-up checklist.

Also see the major discussion of *Business Cards at Conferences*, below.

Conference Notes

Month: _____

Date: _____

Conference: _____

Why are you attending? _____

_____

_____

_____

Goals for this conference: _____

_____

_____

_____

Notes during the conference: _____

_____

_____

_____

Post-conference actions: _____

_____

_____

_____

Additional Notes: _____

_____

_____

_____

Conference Notes

Month: _____

Date: _____

Conference: _____

Why are you attending? _____

_____

_____

_____

Goals for this conference: _____

_____

_____

_____

Notes during the conference: _____

_____

_____

_____

Post-conference actions: _____

_____

_____

_____

Additional Notes: _____

_____

_____

_____

_____

Conference Notes

Month: _____

Date: _____

Conference: _____

Why are you attending? _____

_____

_____

_____

Goals for this conference: _____

_____

_____

_____

Notes during the conference: _____

_____

_____

_____

Post-conference actions: _____

_____

_____

_____

Additional Notes: _____

_____

_____

_____

_____

Conference/Event Evaluation

This evaluation sheet can help you assess in-person events as well as webinars and online conferences. One big question is: Why would you bother? Well, remember, our goal is to work with **intention**. You should have goals for going to events, and goals for putting knowledge to work after events.

In the last section, we set you up to take notes about the conferences you attend. In the next section, we'll do the same for webinars. Here, the task is to build a framework for evaluating what you gained from these events.

Note that this is also a good place to take notes on the overall experience. If you went a day early or stayed a day after, was this a good hotel for that? How was *this* airline with *this* location?

There is also a two-page Event Follow-Up checklist after the event evaluation form.

Event Evaluation Notes

Event (Title): _____

Date: _____

Location: _____

     Notes on Location: _____

Airline: _____

     Notes on this trip: _____

Other transportation: _____

     Notes on transportation: _____

Hotel and Venue: _____

     Notes on Hotel: _____

     Notes on Venue: _____

Was this event useful? Why or why not? _____

_____

Best thing about this event: _____

Worst thing about this event: _____

Best speaker/presenter: _____

Would you return again? _____

If so, every time, in two years, three years, etc.? _____

Sponsors. Which sponsors did you spend time with? _____

_____

_____

Event Evaluation Notes – Continued

What did you learn/gain? _____

_____

_____

Sponsors to follow up with: _____

_____

_____

Sessions you attended: _____

_____

_____

Sessions you missed but want to get recordings of: _____

_____

_____

Overall, what did you accomplish at this event? _____

_____

_____

_____

Additional Notes: _____

_____

_____

_____

Event Evaluation Notes

Event (Title): _____

Date: _____

Location: _____

    Notes on Location: _____

Airline: _____

    Notes on this trip: _____

Other transportation: _____

    Notes on transportation: _____

Hotel and Venue: _____

    Notes on Hotel: _____

    Notes on Venue: _____

Was this event useful? Why or why not? _____

_____

Best thing about this event: _____

Worst thing about this event: _____

Best speaker/presenter: _____

Would you return again? _____

If so, every time, in two years, three years, etc.? _____

Sponsors. Which sponsors did you spend time with? _____

_____

_____

Event Evaluation Notes – Continued

What did you learn/gain? _____

_____

_____

Sponsors to follow up with: _____

_____

_____

Sessions you attended: _____

_____

_____

Sessions you missed but want to get recordings of: _____

_____

_____

Overall, what did you accomplish at this event? _____

_____

_____

_____

Additional Notes: _____

_____

_____

_____

Event Evaluation Notes

Event (Title): _____

Date: _____

Location: _____

    Notes on Location: _____

Airline: _____

    Notes on this trip: _____

Other transportation: _____

    Notes on transportation: _____

Hotel and Venue: _____

    Notes on Hotel: _____

    Notes on Venue: _____

Was this event useful? Why or why not? _____

_____

Best thing about this event: _____

Worst thing about this event: _____

Best speaker/presenter: _____

Would you return again? _____

If so, every time, in two years, three years, etc.? _____

Sponsors. Which sponsors did you spend time with? _____

_____

_____

Event Evaluation Notes – Continued

What did you learn/gain? _____

_____

_____

Sponsors to follow up with: _____

_____

_____

Sessions you attended: _____

_____

_____

Sessions you missed but want to get recordings of: _____

_____

_____

Overall, what did you accomplish at this event? _____

_____

_____

_____

Additional Notes: _____

_____

_____

_____

Event Follow-Up Checklist

Event (Title): _____

Date: _____

☐ Send thank you notes/emails to the following people:

1) _____

    Topic: _____

2) _____

    Topic: _____

3) _____

    Topic: _____

☐ Call to follow up with the following people:

1) _____

    Topic: _____

2) _____

    Topic: _____

3) _____

    Topic: _____

Conference/Event Follow-Up Checklist – Continued

☐ Exchange notes and ideas with the following people who attended sessions you missed:

1) _____

     Session: _____

2) _____

     Session: _____

3) _____

     Session: _____

☐ Mail or email items you promised to people:

Person: _____

     Item/Promise: _____

Person: _____

     Item/Promise: _____

Person: _____

     Item/Promise: _____

☐ Scan business cards into your database, with appropriate notes. (See the lengthy discussion of business cards below.)

☐ Enter next year's event into your calendar, if you plan to attend.

Event Follow-Up Checklist

Event (Title): _____

Date: _____

☐ Send thank you notes/emails to the following people:

1) _____

    Topic: _____

2) _____

    Topic: _____

3) _____

    Topic: _____

☐ Call to follow up with the following people:

1) _____

    Topic: _____

2) _____

    Topic: _____

3) _____

    Topic: _____

Conference/Event Follow-Up Checklist – Continued

☐ Exchange notes and ideas with the following people who attended sessions you missed:

1) _____

      Session: _____

2) _____

      Session: _____

3) _____

      Session: _____

☐ Mail or email items you promised to people:

Person: _____

      Item/Promise: _____

Person: _____

      Item/Promise: _____

Person: _____

      Item/Promise: _____

☐ Scan business cards into your database, with appropriate notes. (See the lengthy discussion of business cards below.)

☐ Enter next year's event into your calendar, if you plan to attend.

Event Follow-Up Checklist

Event (Title): _____

Date: _____

☐ Send thank you notes/emails to the following people:

1) _____

     Topic: _____

2) _____

     Topic: _____

3) _____

     Topic: _____

☐ Call to follow up with the following people:

1) _____

     Topic: _____

2) _____

     Topic: _____

3) _____

     Topic: _____

Conference/Event Follow-Up Checklist – Continued

☐ Exchange notes and ideas with the following people who attended sessions you missed:

1) _____

      Session: _____

2) _____

      Session: _____

3) _____

      Session: _____

☐ Mail or email items you promised to people:

Person: _____

      Item/Promise: _____

Person: _____

      Item/Promise: _____

Person: _____

      Item/Promise: _____

☐ Scan business cards into your database, with appropriate notes. (See the lengthy discussion of business cards below.)

☐ Enter next year's event into your calendar, if you plan to attend.

Quotes . . . to prime your reticular Activating System

"Lack of pep is often mistaken for patience."

— Ken Hubbard

"Let us endeavor so to live that when we die even the undertaker will be sorry."

— Mark Twain

"Life must be lived forwards, but can only be understood backwards."

— Soren Kierkegaard

Webinar Goals for Next Year

Prime Questions

1. As a rule, how useful have you found webinars in the last year? Why?

_____

_____

2. Is there a general brand or kind of webinar that you find the most useful? What is it, and why is this group of webinars better than others?

_____

_____

3. Over the past year, would you say that you attended too many, too few, or just the right number of webinars or online events?

_____

_____

Like conferences and workshops, webinars can be an excellent way to learn new things and keep up to date on trends in business as well as technology. And, like conferences, I encourage you to set both a minimum number you'll attend and a maximum.

Most webinars are about an hour long, so they don't "seem" to take much time, or to be much of a distraction. But that can be deceiving. First, I know that many people put a webinar on one screen while they're doing something else on another. *That is very bad practice!!!* Seriously.

Human beings cannot multi-task. It is literally not possible. The best you can hope for is to pay attention to about 30-70% of each task (and the total cannot add to more than 95% because of the overhead of switching from one task to another). In other words, you are not getting what you can from the webinar AND you're not doing a good job on whatever else you're supposed to be doing.

Webinars also have the disadvantage that they happen on someone else's schedule. That means you need to interrupt whatever you're doing and put your attention on the webinar. Yes, you can tell yourself that you'll listen to the recording, but you probably won't.

I can tell you, after hosting hundreds of webinars over the years, almost no one ever listens to the recordings. On average, about 50-60% of registered attendees actually show up for a free webinar. And less than five percent ever download the recordings. There are exceptions, but very few.

I strongly encourage you to commit to a limited number of webinars – and then give those webinars your complete attention.

If attending a webinar results in **no change of behavior** inside your company, then it has little or no value. As with everything else, you need to consume knowledge, then put it into action. If you constantly consume new information but don't do anything useful with it, you are better off using that time for something else.

How else might you spend your time? Well, an hour's worth of sales calls per week is guaranteed to result in more sales! Or you could spend the hour on billable labor. Or marketing, documentation, or writing standard operating procedures.

If you're going to dedicate your time to webinars, you should have some idea beforehand what you hope to gain. And, afterward, you should digest the information and take some kind of action.

Summary recommendations:

1) Have a reason for attending the webinar. Write it down.

2) Attend – really attend the webinar. Listen. Give it your attention. Take notes.

3) Evaluate the webinar when it's over. What actions will you take as a result? Which web sites will you visit? Who will you email? Will you test-drive a product or service?

Once you commit to stopping and paying attention to a webinar, then you see more clearly that you are taking a valuable hour from your schedule. As a result, I hope you will be a little pickier about attending so many webinars. And, with luck, you will take action based on every webinar you attend.

This workbook contains worksheets for taking advantage of a few webinars. If you attend more, you can always photocopy a page, or print from the download file, and keep track of more.

For evaluation purposes, use the Conference/Event Evaluation above.

Webinar Notes

Month: _____

Date: _____

Webinar: _____

Why are you attending? _____

_____

_____

Goals for this webinar: _____

_____

_____

Notes during the webinar: _____

_____

_____

_____

Post-webinar actions: _____

_____

_____

_____

Additional Notes: _____

_____

_____

_____

_____

Webinar Notes

Month: _____

Date: _____

Webinar: _____

Why are you attending?   _____

_____

_____

Goals for this webinar: _____

_____

_____

Notes during the webinar: _____

_____

_____

_____

Post-webinar actions: _____

_____

_____

_____

Additional Notes: _____

_____

_____

_____

_____

Webinar Notes

Month: _____

Date: _____

Webinar: _____

Why are you attending? _____

_____

_____

Goals for this webinar: _____

_____

_____

Notes during the webinar: _____

_____

_____

_____

Post-webinar actions: _____

_____

_____

_____

Additional Notes: _____

_____

_____

_____

_____

Monthly Tune-Ups

Prime Questions

1. Do you ever have the nagging feeling that you're "forgetting something" when it comes to all the details involved in supporting all of your clients? Explain.

_____

_____

2. Does anyone in your company have the job of constantly fine-tuning your operations or improving your finances? If not you, who is this?

_____

_____

3. Do you have a standardized monthly maintenance that is performed at all clients? Is it customized per client?

_____

_____

Running a business is literally a never-ending job of fixing and tuning and tweaking. If you stop making changes to improve your business, it quickly becomes obsolete. This is truer with technology than any other field!

If you've read my _Managed Services Operations Manual_, you know that I encourage you to create a "Monthly Single" task to execute at all clients, each month. Basically, you choose one big check-up and perform it across all client that month. The goal is to make sure that certain tune-ups take place from time to time, while acknowledging that they do not need to happen every month.

There are three broad categories of tasks that fit into this list. First, there are client-focused jobs. These include things like verifying configurations or test hardware. Second, there are financial items such as keeping office expenses under control. And, third, there items related to you business model (offering, pricing, etc.).

Note: There are more than twelve exercises here. You can combine them if you wish, skip some, double-up in a month, or create a schedule that takes more than twelve months.

For each task, choose someone to be your company lead. This person will customize the task for your company, schedule the work, and either execute or supervise to make sure someone else executes the task. Ideally, they will record the results – and schedule them the remainder of this year, and next year as well.

I've provided a brief description of each. Pick them one at a time and fill out the "Monthly Tune-Up Notes" form. Repeat as needed.

And, of course, create additional tune-up tasks as needed. If you'll be repeating them every year, be sure to add them to next year's task list as well.

There is a "Monthly Tune-Up Notes" form after the proposed monthly Tune-Ups. This should be customized as needed by your organization and the specific task you are addressing.

Monthly Tune-Ups

Task: Create/Update Hardware Sales Card

Month: _____

Description:

In QuickBooks, Xero, Sage, or whatever you use for tracking sales, print out a list of all the **hardware** you sold in the last twelve months. Don't worry about specific part numbers, but just the major categories such as monitors, laptops, firewalls, wireless access points, network cards, etc.

Write out this list, one item per line. Then write the names of your primary and secondary brands for each item.

Note: The fewer total items and brands you sell, the more profitable you will be with each item you sell. Building your sales line card will help focus your service department as well as sales.

Finally, list new items you might sell next year. This might be a specific thing, such as programmable door locks, or a broad category such as IOT devices. If you can make notes on brands, do so. If not, revisit this exercise once you begin actually selling these items.

Task: Create/Update Software Sales Card

Month: _____

Description:

In QuickBooks, Xero, Sage, or whatever you use for tracking sales, print out a list of all the **software** you sold in the last twelve months. Don't worry about specific part numbers, but just the major categories such as Office software, anti-virus, financial packages, graphics suites, etc.

Write out this list, one item per line. Then write the names of your primary and secondary brands for each item. With software, you may only have one brand that you sell.

Note: The fewer total items and brands you sell, the more profitable you will be with each item you sell. Building your sales line card will help focus your service department as well as sales.

Finally, list new items you might sell next year. If you can make notes on brands, do so. If not, revisit this exercise once you begin actually selling these items.

Task: Create/Update Services/Cloud Sales Card

Month: _____

Description:

In QuickBooks, Xero, Sage, or whatever you use for tracking sales, print out a list of all the **hosted services or cloud services** your sold (resold) in the last twelve months. This includes storage, office products, spam filtering, cloud backups, etc.

Write out this list, one item per line. Then write the names of your primary and secondary brands for each item.

Note: The fewer total items and brands you sell, the more profitable you will be with each item you sell. Building your sales line card will help focus your service department as well as sales.

Finally, list new items you might sell next year. If you can make notes on brands, do so. If not, revisit this exercise once you begin actually selling these items.

Task: Fine-Tune the Ticketing System or PSA

Month: _____

Description:

Start by collecting information about your ticketing system or PSA: What is not working quite the way it should? Which features are not implemented? Does it reflect your preferred service model and business model?

Next, assign someone (or more than one) to research, design, and implement changes. This might take longer than a month. But get the process started.

Task: Perform a "Deep Issue Massage" on the Service Board

Month: _____

Description:

The goal here is to clean up the service board. You primarily do this by creating a report view so that 100% of your tickets are visible, and then sort them every way you can. If you determine that you have problems seeing all the tickets, that's a major problem and you need to reconfigure you board to make everything visible.

Sort tickets by status. If you have a status that basically amounts to, "Waiting for the boss to approve this so we can bill or close it," take care of those first. Either force the boss to sit down and take care of this OR bill everything and wait to hear if anyone complains, then close all of them.

Note: Don't pretend that you actually have major issues here, hiding inside your system. You're in this situation because you've been ignoring it for a long time. We're going to put an end to that.

Sort by priority. Do you have a large number of high-priority tickets? If so, what's going on there? Are these real problems, or is the priority system not working the way it should? Do you have a large number of low-priority tickets? If so, are they getting the service they deserve? Make a plan to knock these out.

Sort by client. Are there clients with lots of tickets outstanding? Is that a problem that needs attention?

Sort by ticket age. Do you have a bunch of really old tickets? Are they still necessary? If they're not actually going to get worked, how will you make note of the fact that you have problems that don't need solving?

And so forth. Literally sort and resort your tickets any way you can. Do it again. The result will be: 1) You will eliminate tickets that are no longer needed. As a result, every ticket in your system will be "real." 2) Your system will be clean and will be a lot more useful because it represents what's actually going on in your service department. 3) Now the service manager can perform a light massage every Monday and keep the system clean.

Task: Tune Up the RMM Settings

Month: _____

Description:

Start by collecting information about your RMM. Is it reporting the right information and not under-reporting problems? What is not working quite the way it should? Which features are not implemented? Does it reflect your preferred service model and business model?

Next, assign someone (or more than one) to research, design, and implement changes. This might take longer than a month. But get the process started.

Task: Evaluate Your Anti-Virus and Malware Solution

Month: _____

Description:

Note: This might be an every-other-year task. Or maybe even every three years.

I'm not a fan of changing major tools, especially those that have become commodities. Review your AV and Malware solution. In particular, look at what you are paying and how it's performing.

Are you using the tool that ships with your RMM? If so, there is a default case to keep this tool because it is easy to monitor and deploy. If not, compare your current solution to the one that ships with your RMM. Again, if you're going to make a change, that is probably the default first choice.

Don't get hung up on which tool had some problem in the last twelve months. Eventually, they will all have problems. If your preferred tool had several problems in the last twelve months, that's a legitimate reason to consider switching.

Task: Evaluate Your SOC (Security Operations Center)

Month: _____

Description:

> Do you use a SOC? If not, is it time to choose one? If so, are you getting the service and support you need? In the ever-escalating world of ransomware, does your SOC provide the level of security and support you need to feel that your clients are protected?

> Any other considerations around the performance of your SOC?

> If you choose to seek another solution, define some specific criteria and assign someone to do the research. This process may take more than a month.

Task: Evaluate Your BDR (Backup and Disaster Recovery) Solution

Month: _____

Description:

> Is your current BDR offering working well? Is it easy to manage and to verify that it's working? Do you perform monthly restores to verify that all of your technicians know how to use it?

> Are there other alternatives you should be looking at (for example, cloud-only solutions)? How do the service and price of your current solution compare to alternatives available today?

> If you choose to seek another solution, define some specific criteria and assign someone to do the research. This process may take more than a month.

Task: Evaluate Your Cloud Services Distributor

Month: _____

Description:

> Where do you buy most of your cloud services? See the notes on creating a sales line card: Have you minimized the number of vendors you have to go to for cloud services? If you have too many vendors, are you really running the most efficient operation you can?

> Evaluate each cloud vendor. What do you buy from them? What could you buy from them? Is there a reason for not consolidating the number of vendors?

> If you choose to combine services or make changes in your service offering, define some specific criteria and assign someone to do the research. You will need a plan to make the transition. This process will take more than a month.

Task: Backup All Client Documentation

Month: _____

Description:

> If you do not have a clear, documented process for documenting your clients' operations, you need one. Begin creating that process. This may take a while.

> If you do have a good client documentation process, great. You also need to back it up. Ideally, there should be some easily-readable report that you can give to each client. It might be on a USB key or stored in a ZIP file on their cloud drive (in an extremely safe place).

> Think about the worst-case scenario: Their office burns down and their cloud storage vendor goes out of business. And the client can't get ahold of you for whatever reason. How will the client get usable documentation so they can start rebuilding their business?

> I recommend something physical like a USB key that can go into a file box with their end-of-year finances and be sent off to secure storage.

Task: Backup All Internal Documentation

Month: _____

Description:

> See the previous item. You need to do exactly the same with your internal documentation. This is the ultimate disaster recovery. You can't imagine the impossible scenario – until it happens.

Task: Evaluate Preferred Distributors

Month: _____

Description:

> This is another item that might be an every other year or every three years activity.
>
> I recommend that you have two primary distributors. You may want to have just one, but that can cause problems. With two distributors, you can do at least the minimal price comparison. Checking six distributors often takes more time (which is money) than it's worth.
>
> With two distributors, you can order enough from each so that you maintain decent pricing. And then, when you have a problem with one distributor, you can buy everything from the other until the problem is solved. If you keep giving the problem distributor your money, they aren't very motivated to solve the problem.
>
> Let your distributors know that you are auditing relationships to make sure you are getting consistently good prices and service. Who knows, you might get a dedicated sales team or some other perk out of it.

Task: Tweak your business model

Month: _____

Description:

> This is a big one. Evaluate your business model. Should you be selling more or less hardware? Should you be pushing projects or moving away from them? Should you use a flat-fee maintenance model? Should you be a high-end concierge service?
>
> All year long, you attend webinars and seminars. You read books and take classes. You learn all kinds of stuff related to your business. But do you actually make changes? Do you integrate information so that it improves your business model?
>
> It should! And it's not always easy. So I don't want to pretend it is. But, at some point, you need to sit down and look at the big picture. Is your business operating in a way that will be successful in 2025 or 2030?
>
> I know the future is sometimes hard to see. But if there are major trends, you should be aware of them and make conscious decisions about implementing new processes – or not. Act with intention.

Task: Which emerging technologies should you be implementing?

Month: _____

Description:

> We've looked at hardware, software, and services. So some of this topic is covered there. But now let's look at true "emerging" technologies. You can always Google "CompTIA top 10 emerging technologies" for a great list of things to consider.
>
> Some of these (like blockchain or biometrics) may feel outside your business model. Okay. But at least spend a bit of time thinking about them. Others (such as serverless computing and 5G) seem much more obvious. But what do they look like in the real world with your customers?

Task: Refresh your web site

Month: _____

Description:

> This is an easy one. If you haven't refreshed your web site in three years, now's the time. It does NOT have to be amazing, cutting-edge or expensive. But it should look modern.

> When prospects check you out, you should look competent and professional. All the links should work. Your picture should be up to date. The icons should look like "what the kids are doing these days."

> Most small businesses have small, static web sites. They don't have to compete with Disney or IBM. But they should look good enough for a client to choose to engage.

Task: Quarterly marketing goals

Month: _____

Description:

> If you haven't done so already NOW is always a great time to start laying out marketing goals for the next four quarters. That means newsletter, social media, and other promotions. You should have a marketing calendar. What will you do in Q1? Q2? etc. Here's an example:

> Q1 Marketing

> - Three newsletters
> - One mailing campaign: 500 manufacturers in the metro area
> - Six blog posts
> - Post on social media three times per week (Facebook, LinkedIn)

This task is worth doing simply because it probably won't get done unless it's spelled out, written down, and assigned to someone. And it needs to be done!

Task: Quarterly advertising goals

Month: _____

Description:

> See the previous item. But note: Marketing is not sales! Advertising should be sales-focused, not marketing-focused. Sales means asking someone for their money. It means asking someone to engage with you. The call to action is not "read my newsletter," but is **buy my stuff!**

> Like marketing, you should have a calendar for advertising. Unlike marketing, which *may* have a budget, sales *must* have a budget. Sales also needs to have a measurable return on investment.

> I recommend that you have a consistent budget every month. Half of it should be spent on the same thing all year (such as Google ads). The other half should be spent trying new things, such as an ad with the local chamber of commerce or Facebook ads.

> Define a quarterly budget and sales activity calendar.

Task (Defined by you): _____

Month: _____

Description:

> Define your task. Be as specific as possible. If you need to, write out why you need to do this. Also, will you be assigning this task to someone in particular? And will it be completed in this month, or will it take longer?

> The more detail the better.

[Author's Note: If you have really good ideas that I failed to list above, please let me know so I can update future workbooks. Email karlp@smallbizthoughts.com]

Quotes . . . to prime your reticular Activating System

"Miracles are achieved when we get beyond our own perceived limitations."

— Wayne Dyer, Real Magic

"Modesty in human beings is praised because it is not a matter of nature, but of will."

— Lactantius

"More people would learn from their mistakes if they weren't so busy denying that they made them."

— Anonymous

Monthly Tune-Up Notes

Task: _____

Month: _____

This Tune-Up Assigned to: _____

Customized as of: _____

Notes on work done: _____

_____

_____

_____

_____

_____

_____

_____

_____

_____

_____

Documentation is completed _____

Documentation stored at: _____

_____

_____

_____

_____

_____

Monthly Tune-Up Notes

Task: _____

Month: _____

This Tune-Up Assigned to: _____

Customized as of: _____

Notes on work done: _____

_____

_____

_____

_____

_____

_____

_____

_____

_____

_____

Documentation is completed   _____

Documentation stored at: _____

_____

_____

_____

_____

_____

Monthly Tune-Up Notes

Task: _____

Month: _____

This Tune-Up Assigned to: _____

Customized as of: _____

Notes on work done: _____

_____

_____

_____

_____

_____

_____

_____

_____

_____

_____

_____

Documentation is completed   _____

Documentation stored at: _____

_____

_____

_____

_____

Embrace Outsourcing from Now On

Prime Questions

1. How much have you relied on outsourced resources for your business? Will this change in the year ahead?

_____

_____

2. As a rule do you consider outsourced resources to be lower-quality or higher-quality than the talent you have in-house?

_____

_____

3. How open are you to expanding the capabilities of your company by relying on contractors or outsourced personnel?

_____

_____

We've all been in the "outsourced IT" business for a long time. It basically defines who we are to our clients. And, truth be told, most of us have outsourced some of our labor to others as well. The world of outsourcing – and remote outsourcing in particular – has grown dramatically in the last ten years.

I can honestly declare that the "outsource" market is mature. As long as you follow the laws regarding how you pay people, and take care of the taxes, it can be a great way to increase your capacity and reduce your overhead. But you also have to set some standards and make sure they're followed.

My experience managing outsourced labor started a long time ago. I managed the technical side of the work-from-home program for HP's Roseville, CA plant in 1995-1996. I didn't manage any of those remote workers, but my team configured and serviced the laptop (and desktop) machines that were used by remote workers. Prior to that I had been a remote worker, managing employees in three states even while I traveled. So, my personal remote experience goes all the way back to 1993.

[Insert old man stories about the equipment we used back then.]

But as far as managing people for my own company, that evolved in the 2000's. Some of it was the standard business of working with my own technicians on the other side of town. But then we quickly evolved to have a help desk in India (via Zenith Infotech, now Continuum), higher-end support from Microsoft MVPs we had contracted with, graphics people and web developers in the U.S. and Philippines, and so forth.

I think I will have done remote assistance of one kind or another forever. After all, why should a web designer, SQL programmer, or social media assistant have to come to my office? The truth is, they are probably more efficient and effective from their home base.

Here's a quick overview of the kinds of resources you can outsource today. This is the tip of the iceberg, of course. But it will get you started.

<u>Remote employees.</u> Okay, if they're real employees, they are not really outsourced. But they need to be managed almost identically.

<u>1099 (contract) workers.</u> Many people don't consider these folks outsourced either. But if they're not your actual employees, contract workers are the very definition of outsourced employees.

<u>Virtual specialists.</u> This includes "virtual assistants" (VAs) of all stripes. Some are primarily office administrative assistants. But some are also bookkeepers, accountants, graphics professionals, layout artists, copywriters for advertising, marketing companies, etc.

There's a big bucket that falls under the term VA, but there really are a lot of specialists. I outsource two different graphics people, each of whom specializes in specific services. I also have people who perform very specific services related to book publishing. And, of course, I've used help desk and escalation services such as Third Tier.

These outsourced resources can be divided into three broad kinds of businesses. First, there are individuals who provide their specific skill set, generally for an hourly fee. Second, there are small companies (1-10 employees) that will provide services. These usually have one primary person you deal with. And, third, there are larger companies. These tend to be the big, faceless companies that we all know, such as SalesForce.com or Intuit.

Some Resources

Looking to find outsource opportunities for your business? Here are a few places to start. First, let's look at "generic" resources that any business could use. Then we'll look at IT or MSP-specific resources.

Any business might find value in these outsourced resources:

❖ **Upwork** - www.upwork.com

This is the ultimate place to find pretty much anything you want. I have used Upwork to find SQL programmers, web designers, video editors, graphics designers, voice over artists, and more. You can filter by talent, country, cost, and many more options. If nothing else, it's worth browsing this web site to see what's available.

❖ **Fiverr.com**

I have come to rely heavily on Fiverr for creative work. If I have an idea for a graphic, I can create a very rough draft. But I'm not an artist or Photoshop guru. So I hire someone at Fiverr for less than $100 and get amazing stuff. Take a look around and see which resources you might be able to hire at a very reasonable price.

❖ **Craigslist.org**

Hey, don't laugh. It's actually amazing who you will find on CL. I have hired several "local" web designers over the last fifteen years from CL. Only two of them ever came and worked in my office. The others worked from home and were totally outsourced. I just happen to find them through CL. Remember, just because you want to outsource doesn't mean they have to live in another country.

❖ **Referrals**

My primary book cover designer, my primary virtual assistant, my transcriptionist, and the person who does all my book layouts came to me as referrals. In other words, I asked someone in a meeting, on social media, or in a mastermind group if they knew someone. You want work through referrals, right? Well, so do lots of other good people.

Now let's look at a few IT-specific recommendations.

❖ **Third Tier (www.thirdtier.net)**

If you're in IT and you get stuck, you have about three options: 1) Call the hardware vendor support line; 2) Call the software vendor support line; or 3) Call Third Tier. They have a stable of really smart people who can handle pretty much any problem you've got. Don't know PowerShell? They do. Afraid of Azure Active Directory? They're not.

You get the point. Sometimes you're just too busy or overwhelmed. A couple years ago, I had a client with an Exchange issue and I had jury duty. I probably could have got out of jury duty, but I put in a ticket with Third Tier and they just handled it.

❖ **Continuum by ConnectWise (www.continuum.net)**

Okay, you need to be a Continuum RMM subscriber to take advantage of their help desk. But if you are a subscriber, please be sure to use this service! They do some amazing work. Even little stuff like analyzing blue screens. You look at two a year. They have a team that does nothing else! Trust me, they'll find the problem faster than you.

❖ **Other Outsourced Help Desk**

As for other options, this is a growing market. Google " helpdesk for msp outsource " to see. The prices are going down, down, down. You could potentially have a business where all you do it take support tickets and assign them to someone else, paying a flat fee per month.

Rules for Managing Outsourced Labor

We've talked about some of the things you can outsource and shared some places to get started. Now lets cover some basic rules for actually managing outsourced resources and give some ideas about things you cannot outsource.

Interestingly enough, managing outsourced "resources" is a lot like managing in-house employees in your office. After all, they are people who need to communicate with you, and potentially with your clients. They need to perform tasks efficiently. And they need to report back to you.

If any of that fails, it's partly your fault. Just like any other employee.

I only have a few rules for managing outsourced resources. They are all in support of the goals just stated.

1) Be very clear what you want. You have to define the desired outcome in order for someone to be successful. It might be to call down this list of prospects, configure a firewall, install a printer remotely, or produce marketing graphics. It could be just about anything, but you need to be super clear what you want.

Example: You cannot assign a task that simply says, "Fix the Router." Just as with your own technicians, you need to define the problem and the desired outcome. And the more steps you give them the better. In some cases, you might say that you don't know what the problem is.

Maybe port 3389 looks open but you're not getting a response via RDP. Tell them everything you know.

At other times, you might know exactly what you want but you just don't want to do it yourself. For example, you want them to open a specific port, forward it to an internal machine, and verify that they can access the resource there. Of course, you'll also want them to back up the configuration before they start and after they finish - to a specific location.

2) Define one task per request. Just as you do with your ticketing system, you need one task per request. This is especially true if you are connecting primarily via email. It becomes a disaster if you have seven tasks in a massive email string that gets longer and longer as you work your way through totally unrelated activities. A ticketing system is preferred.

Use a good "title" or short description. Then have a clear longer description of what you want. For Example:

> Subject: Call Down for Lunch-and-Learn
>
> Content: Download the "Friday Lunch-and-Learn Chamber" Excel spreadsheet. Add a column for your notes and comments. Call each person on the list using the script on the second worksheet. Add Yes, No, and Maybe notes to the attendee worksheet. Let me know if you have any questions. Due by Wednesday at 5 PM Pacific time.

3) Agree on Reporting. How will the outsourced resource report to you? Email? Via your CRM logon? Inside the Upwork tool? On a shared drive Excel spreadsheet?

This is particularly true of longer projects. If you use email, also use some kind of filters so their email doesn't go missing. You can filter outsourced resource emails into a specific folder within your "inbox" - or whatever works for you.

Remember, reporting goes both ways. When they ask for feedback or clarification, don't wait a week. You'll start wondering what they're up to and they'll start wondering if you really want the work done. As I mentioned above, management comes down to actively managing.

Related to this: You need to hold your virtual employees/contractors accountable for what they agreed on. You need to hold up your side of the communication system, and they need to hold up theirs. If they're good, they'll be busy. So you need to work on making sure you agree on timing and feedback.

4) Agree on Data Exchange. Everyone has a place in the cloud where they want to store stuff and exchange information. You need to be in control of which tools you use. If they throw something on an insecure, free hosted drive, you have no idea how secure your data are. You need to have a tool and you need to give them access. In some cases, that costs money.

Go slow. Be careful. Make sure you all agree on where things get put or exchanged. I'm not a fan of email for this stuff, but lots of people still use it.

5) Use checklists whenever you can. Whether it's configuring a firewall or agreeing on graphic design, the more you can define exactly what you need and the order you need it, the better.

Humans have an amazing capacity to assume information that is not present. We literally fill in the blanks. You might assume that "anyone" would do it your way. But someone else might ask why you think *this* is related to *that*. To combat this, it's your job as the manager to fill in the blanks and be as clear as possible.

Good outsourced resources might have their own checklists. They will also help you refine yours. The result is a process that becomes easier and easier to outsource with better results. Embrace the checklist mentality!

6) Pay promptly. Whether you pay by PayPal, check, ECH, or credit card, pay promptly! People who work virtually are almost always independent contractors and small businesses. They are not large corporations. You want to be paid promptly. So do they.

You already know this, so I won't go on and on. Just do it. It's great for the relationship.

What Can't Be Outsourced?

A few years ago, I posted an ad for an in-house administrative assistant. In the ad, I said please don't reply if you're not in Sacramento. OMG! This opened an amazing storm of virtual assistants pummeling me with complaints that I don't understand how much they can do.

One even said she could do my filing. If I sent her the paperwork and the file cabinet, she would send it back in perfect condition, perfectly filed.

OK.

I hope she understands how thoroughly absurd that is. There are MANY things you need to outsource to a real human being who lives in your town. Maybe you need an employee. Or maybe you need a contractor.

Remember: Outsourcing does not mean you are sending work to another state or country! If I have enough things to do over a long period of time, I will probably hire someone. But sometimes I need three or four different people to get all these things done. In that case, I will probably hire each of them separately as contractors.

Here's the list of things I **don't** outsource over the Internet:

- Filing papers in my file cabinet
- Putting gas in my car
- Scanning business cards into my database (This could be sent to a remote V.A., but I'd either have to ship the cards or scan them and send a PDF, so it's not worth it.)
- Tiny jobs such as postal mailing a letter or box
- Packing my signs and handouts for a trip
- Print handouts, build folders, prepare name tags, etc.
- Install network cards (hard drives, memory, etc.)
- Onsite prospect network evaluations

Obviously, the list goes on. The point is, you should make these lists. You should list out the things you CAN outsource. Once you begin outsourcing, you will find that you can do more than you thought.

Remember: You are someone else's outsourced resource. They hire you so they don't have to hire a technician in-house.

This is the future economy. There is massive talent all over the globe, being connected more and more every day.

Outsourcing allows all of us to get more done, expand our offerings, expand our work hours, reduce our costs, and even help us get into new markets. Once you start delegating beyond your employees, you see that you really can expand your business dramatically!

Some people give me a bad time for sending programming work to India and the Philippines, or for using Fiverr for finding graphic artists. All I can say is that I have access to amazing talent at a reasonable price. They're happy. I'm happy. And I think outsourcing will continue to be a growing part of our national and global economies going forward.

Expand what your company can do today and in the future: Embrace Outsourcing!

Should You Hire or Outsource Technicians?

One of the biggest steps you go through as your company grows is whether you should hire or outsource a technician. After that, you need to decide whether you should get someone full time or part time.

Fundamentally, this is a challenge of cashflow.

It's critical to remember that no technician will ever be 100% billable. So you have to accept the fact that there is some management, some training, some downtime, etc.

I made a video to address some things to consider. Go to my YouTube channel at https://www.youtube.com/smallbizthoughts and search for "SOP: Hire vs. Outsource."

One option is to start with a part time employee. That's great for you, but hard for the technician. So, don't be surprised if they leave for a more full time job. Hiring an employee makes it easy for you to make sure the taxes are paid properly.

Outsourcing is attractive because the engagement can be very limited in scope. Just make sure you sign an agreement so that all three parties (you, the technician, and the tax man) know exactly what the relationship is.

Very often, the hourly cost for these options comes out about the same. But there are lots of variables to consider as you grow.

The Concept of "Team" in the Gig Economy

As the years roll on, I am struck by the amazing team I work with.

I also had an amazing team ten years ago, but it was very different. Back then, my team consisted of twelve people and about half a million dollars in payroll. I had an office staff, technicians, graphics designer, dedicated programmer, and lots of administrative assistants.

Fifteen years before that, I managed a team of more than twenty-five people, broken into three primary responsibility roles. Each individual team consisted of specialists who excelled at one thing

Today I have two employees on payroll. My administrative assistants are outsourced. I work with two accountants, both outsourced. I have two web programmers and two graphics people – all of them outsourced. When needed, I hire specialty programmers, voice over talent, layout designers, and UI designers. And, of course, I outsource some instructors for our five-week classes.

Today my team is about twelve people. But total expenses and payroll are under $100,000. I also have a life coach, who doesn't "work for me" per se. But she helps me make good decisions.

Finally, I have three different unofficial advisory boards in the mastermind groups I belong to. These are all unpaid. But we help each other out, keep each other in line with our stated goals, and brainstorm about the future.

I loved the days when I saw my team every day. I loved walking into the office with a new scheme to change the business or develop a new product. Work would be delegated quickly and everyone buzzed around making stuff happen. And my team loved being my team. It was a great time.

Today I am probably more productive and certainly more "lean" than ever. Most members of my current team have never met each other in real life. In fact, there's a few I've never met in real life. But it works.

It's important to think of your team as a team - whether they're local or remote. You need to conceptualize them as a team in order to maintain a picture of the Big Picture. You also need to recognize that most members of your remote team don't see themselves that way. They see you as a client and only know your business in terms of your interaction with them.

You need this centralized vision in order to maintain your branding to the outside world. And choosing outsourced resources is just as important as choosing employees. You need to remember to hire based on your overall culture and fit with the branding you want the rest of the world to see.

I firmly believe that most IT consultants will find themselves down-sizing their teams while taking on more clients in the years ahead. We really are the masters of automation, if we choose to be.

If you haven't broken out of an IT service business model that emerged fifty years ago, maybe this is the year to consider how "else" you can run your business.

Quotes . . . to prime your reticular Activating System

"Nothing great was ever done without much enduring."

— Saint Catherine of Siena

"Oh, it's delightful to have ambitions. I'm so glad I have such a lot. And there never seems to be any end to them—that's the best of it. Just as soon as you attain to one ambition you see another one glittering higher up still. It does make life so interesting."

— Anne of Green Gables by L.M. Montgomery

"One never finds life worth living. One always has to make it worth living."

— Harry Emerson Fosdick

Business Cards at Conferences

Prime Questions

1. Do you intentionally take business cards to conferences, or show up without them? Why?

_____

_____

2. Do your consider your business cards to be a marketing resource, a necessary (evil) expense, or something in the middle?

_____

_____

3. Do you collect business cards when you go to meetings? If so, do you actually do anything with them?

_____

_____

This section starts with a lot of notes about business cards, how to use them, and how not to use them. Then we have some forms related to "cleaning up" after a conference.

First, my **very opinionated** view of business cards . . .

I find business cards very frustrating. Maybe 75% of the people with business cards should never have them because 1) They never need them due to the nature of their job, 2) They don't know how to use them, or 3) Their cards are almost useless.

On the first point, there are lots of people who just go to the office and are never out meeting people or representing the company. Other than to show their parents, or pass out as "dating cards," these people never use their business cards. So, get these folks 100 or so and don't worry about the cost per card because they'll never need another 100.

How To Use A Business Card (and Why Your Business Card Might be Useless)

At gatherings I almost always collect business cards. That is, I do if I have a reason to. Believe it or not, I don't put everyone I've ever met on my mailing list. When I collect a card, I either intend to contact that person or (on occasion) I intend to add them to a list.

Here's an exercise. Take out your business card. Turn it over and write on the back:

> 1=Small Biz Mixer
>
> 2=Kid is soccer league
>
> 3=Send seminar invite

That's a sample of the kind of notes I might put on the back of your card after meeting you at a conference.

If you can't write this on the back of your card, neither can anyone else! If that's the case, order new business cards. If the back of your cards is glossy, throw them away and order new business cards. If the back of your card is covered with advertising or something else, throw them away and order new business cards.

I hear this ridiculous advice over and over: "You should use the back of your business card (so it's not wasted)." Bullshit. You should leave the back of your card empty enough for me to write some critical information.

As someone who really uses the cards I collect, I want that space on the back of every card. You can use some of the space for YOU (info, logo, QR code, etc.), but leave most of the space for ME. I have databases totaling about 25,000 business cards I've collected over the years. These are for personal contacts, IT consultants, potential clients, authors and speakers, services I might buy, etc.

When I come back to the office with a fist full of business cards, they need to be processed. What does that mean? It means that I put them into piles. Some I throw away. Some are very important. Some I promised to send a link or an article. A few I promised an email. Some I want to pitch an idea to. All of the "keepers" are given to an admin to scan into a database. (See more below.)

You get the idea.

1) They need to be sorted into appropriate piles

2) Some of them require follow-up

ALL of them need a note about where I met the person, the circumstances, and anything interesting about that connection. Where do I write those notes? On the Back of The Business Card!

Oh, but wait. There's crap all over the back of the card. It's dark colored, or has a graphic, or a table, it's glossy, or it has a list of useless links. The point is: I can't write on the back of the card if there's no place to write!

Seriously. There are people who collect your business cards and people who don't. The people who don't collect cards don't matter. Period. They will never see the back of your card.

The people who DO collect business cards are pretty consistent in their behavior: They turn it over and write a note about where they met you, when they met you, notes about what they promised you, and other miscellaneous notes.

Now it's up to you: Will you give them a place to write the notes, or will you take it up with self-serving gimmicks that only waste space?

Business Card Don'ts

Do not print your business card sideways. I believe that 90% of the people who collect business cards will not take you seriously. Some (me included), will simply throw them away.

I guess people think the business card is an opportunity for self-expression, creativity, etc. That's fine. But you don't print your business letters or your letterhead in landscape format on legal size paper. Why? Because it's just not done that way. We live in a society where business forms are determined by the norms set down by others. Get over it.

Your marketing adviser might think that sideways printing makes you stand out and be unique. They're wrong. It's not unique. It's not clever. It's not different enough to make you look like a Maverick Brainiac. If you want to stand out, change your name to an unpronounceable symbol. But print your business cards like a business professional!

Remember:

There are people who collect your business cards and people who don't. The people who don't collect cards don't matter. The people who collect business cards expect a normal card. Give it to them.

Do not use Laser Perf business cards. First, . . . It doesn't matter what's first. Don't do it! Second, let's say you are a professional. Professionals look professional. And they need to look particularly professional with the things that people might associate with your profession.

Computer-printed cards are 99.99% less professional than real business cards. "Free" cards from Vista Print with a logo on the back are better than laser perf. With shipping, your cost is about $.05 per card. Laser perf cards are about $.05 per card.

A recent Google search returned *more than six billion* hits for the term Business Cards. And there are more places than that. Staples has in-house printing. 1,000 cards will cost you about $.03 per card - or less. The point is: Laser perf cards are not any cheaper than real, professional cards. AND they look cheap.

And they feel cheap.

If you use high volume, the cards get cheaper and cheaper. Five billion of those online printers will also bargain with you to lower the price more, if you contact them directly or order cards for everyone in the office.

Remember:

There are people who collect your business cards and people who don't. The people who don't collect cards don't matter. The people who collect business cards will make fun of you if you have a laser perf card.

Do not have a glossy back on your business cards. See the discussion above. Take it to heart. Most of the time when I am handed a glossy-backed card, I try to write on the back and can't. This does two things. First, it makes you fish around for some other way to give me a writing surface or pen that might work. Second, it totally derails the conversation. Now instead of listening to your elevator speech, we're talking about your stupid business cards.

The lesson: Glossy-backed cards are completely useless. Okay. To be fair, they're useful to people who only scan cards into a database. And completely useless to the other 95% of the people you hand a card to.

A while back, I was in a conversation where one person was giving a card to another person so he could mail something they were talking about. Glossy back. We all brought out pens and pencils to see if anything worked. Finally, I brought out one of my business cards and he wrote the message on that. Then the two cards were folded together so the recipient would remember to send the item to the person whose card was with mine.

Remember:

There are people who collect your business cards and people who don't. The people who don't collect cards don't matter. The people who collect business cards will be really disappointed that you have a glossy card.

Do not use reverse print or obnoxious color combinations on your business cards. You've seen it. Dark red background with lime green ink. Your eyes take a minute to focus. Then the type begins to move. Pretty soon you have vertigo. And invariably the business is something like "Creative Solutions." Really? How about changing your company name to Stupid Decisions or Bad Examples?

Business cards should be functional. Think of the context. You hand your card to someone and they need to quickly get enough information off of it to engage you in a discussion. They might write a note on the back. Then it goes into their pocket until it is processed and scanned.

Unless you actually have black light-enabled cards and hand them out in bars, the reverse printing is just annoying. Our brains don't work like that. Make it readable. Make it useful.

Business Card Do's

Okay, enough complaining. How about a checklist that is useful for constructing and using business cards? Great. Start here.

1. Your Name (you personally) should be clear and visible and readable from arm's length.

That means it is also easy to find. Everyone hates a business card with strange font combinations so you have to scan all over the card to find the person's name. Where's Waldo? Or whoever I'm talking to.

2. Your Company name should be clear and easy to find.

3. Contact information is up to you.

Some cards only have email or only have a phone number. It depends on how you want to be contacted. If you want to give your entire mailing address and phone extension, that's fine. Decide WHY you would hand out this information and what you really need on that card to fulfill your needs.

I know I'm not normal, but I never answer my phone. It's not my preferred means of communication. As a result, I don't put my phone number on my business card. It would confuse people who think that they can call that number and get a response.

4. Company logo and slogan.

If you have a nice logo or a slogan that really helps you differentiate yourself, then find a place for them on your card. Remember: They should contribute to the goal of making your card useful and easy to use. If they detract, get them out of the way, make them smaller, move them to the side, or drop them altogether.

5. Titles . . . hmmmmm.

Some people need titles. But most of us don't really need titles on our cards. They're just one more thing that needs to be changed if you change jobs. I don't put titles on my cards. Does a title do something for you? If yes, put it on the card. If not, leave it off.

Sometimes we feel obligated to put something on the card for a title. If so, make it descriptive and useful. Or bland and boring. But whatever you do, do it intentionally and not because you feel you need to put something there.

6. Other Information (QR Code, Facebook Page, LinkedIn, Twitter-X, Pinterest, Yelp, Reddit, Technorati, StumbledUpon, Digg, Yahoo Instant Messenger, Jagg, blog, Klout, TikTok, Instagram, 4Square, etc.).

I bet you know where this is going.

There is simply too much miscellaneous stuff to fit it all on a tiny little business card. So, if you want to put something else on there, be picky. Choose a few things that don't take up much space AND that contribute to your marketing goals.

7. Use the back Wisely. Or leave it blank.

Remember, the back of the card is not for ten little tips, quotations, IP Subnet calculators, etc. The back is primarily for notes. You can use some of the back for links, logos, QR code, etc. But leave at least half of it blank - or lined for notes.

8. Make your business card scannable. You should have a business card scanner, or an app on your phone that scans cards. If not, visit your more successful competition and borrow theirs. Make sure that your business card is clean and clear enough that it scans well.

This little tip will go a long way to making sure you've addressed several of the points in this section. The fonts and colors won't be crazy. The text is actually legible. The card is printed correctly (not sideways). And so forth.

In the 2020's, there's a lot of wisdom in creating a resume that is primarily intended for computers to consume rather than humans. It is the same with business cards. You might hand your card to a human, or drop it in a vendor bucket. But the real value comes when that card gets scanned and someone enters it (you) into their contact database. If it's difficult to process, it's likely to be discarded.

How To Buy Business Cards

If your local printer can compete with online digital printers, great. If not, go find an online place you like. I've had both good and bad experiences with Vista Print. I have to say that their cards are first rate with regard to paper. And I like the default "flat" finish. It can be hard to get printers to understand that you want a glossy front and a flat back.

I have used OvernightPrints.com several times and been very pleased. Even if they do something wrong, they fix it no questions asked and super fast. They have a variety of downloadable templates (MS Word, Adobe Illustrator, etc.). I also like uprinting.com because they do a nice job with rounded corners and interesting die cuts. Just make sure you pick a shape that will successfully go through a business card scanner!

If you are not proficient enough to use Publisher, Illustrator, or some other program to design business cards, please hire someone who is. Upwork.com, 99designs.com, and a million other places can get this done for cheap. You might even hire an intern from the local design school for $20/hr. It's more than they would make working for McDonald's, and it builds their portfolio.

Many sites (most sites?) have wizards so you can create your cards online. Click-click-click and you're done. Upload your logo and away you go. Generally speaking, if you produce your own design, you will upload it as a PDF file. Be sure to embed the fonts so it doesn't get kicked back to you.

Organize Your Business Cards

I know this will shock you if you're a regular reader of my blog, but we have a standard location for all business cards and related files. On our primary drive, it's under \Marketing\Business Cards. That's where we keep copies of the source files, source graphics, QR codes, etc. Illustrator and PDF files are named after the person with a date embedded in the name. e.g., "Biz_Card_KarlP_20250130.pdf" We use the underscore in case spaces cause a problem with the machine we're uploading to.

Keeping all your cards in one place makes it easy to create new cards that are completely consistent with everyone else in the company. It also makes it easy to change formats for all cards if you make a company-wide change. If you have a generational change like that, you should put the old format into a sub-directory.

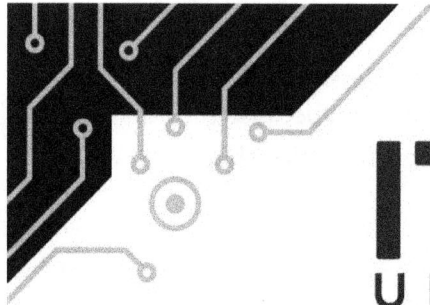

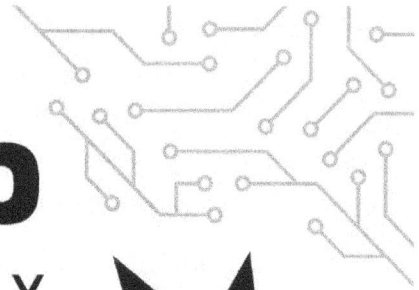

ITSP UNIVERSITY

Great Classes since 2013 !

IT Service Provider University delivers training by Industry Experts to improve your professionalism and your bottom line.

To help fill the gaps between being an IT Professional and successful business owner.

- Automation
- Cloud Services
- Entrepreneurship
- Financial Processes
- Hiring & Training
- Managed Services
- Management
- Marketing
- Office Admin
- Organize Your Business
- QuickBooks
- Sales
- Selling an MSP
- Service Agreements
- SOPs
- Sustainable Growth
- Tools (PSA, RMM, etc.)

And Certifications!

Certification demonstrates your professionalism and commitment to your client's success.

Demonstrate knowledge of the managed service business model and how it is implemented in the real world.

Five pathways to certification.

* Service Management * Technician *
* Front Office * Management *
* Sales * Marketing*

IT Service Provider University

ITSPU.com

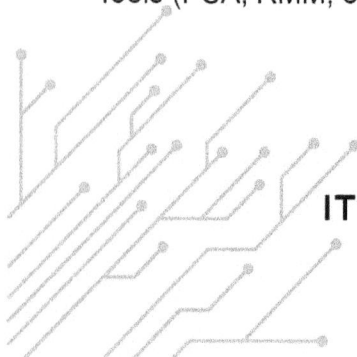
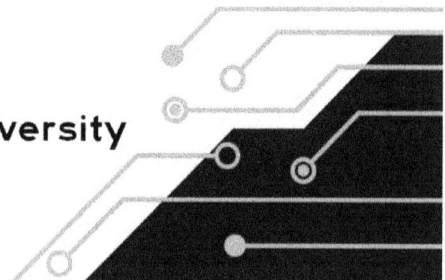

Monthly Financial Kick in the Butt

Prime Questions

1. What is your relationship with money? Do you feel bad or greedy when you focus on money?

_____

_____

2. How often do you review "the big picture" of your business finances?

_____

_____

3. Did you have financial surprises in the last year that you did not anticipate (whether good or bad)?

_____

_____

Here's the final exercise for this workbook. I highly encourage you to take time every month to consider the month ahead. Ideally, you will do this on the last few days of the previous month. So, in the days between Christmas and New Year's, take some time and think about January.

If you follow my **Relax Focus Succeed** blog and newsletter, you know that I consider sitting in a chair and doing nothing fifteen minutes per day to be the highest value activity in my life and business. For this monthly sit-down with yourself, I encourage you to take 30-60 minutes to dedicate some time thinking about your business.

How is it going? How has the month been? What needs to be done in the month ahead?

My friend Stacey Powell is a financial advisor. She encourages me to literally light a candle and spend an hour every month looking at my finances. The candle is all about taking this seriously and making a bit of a ceremony out of the experience. (I have to admit, I sometimes light candles for no good reason, but I don't do it for finances.)

Her book is: _The Finance Gym Action Plan for a Better Life with Money: Don't just know better. Do better._ You can find it on Amazon for less than $30.

What *I* want you to do every month is basically take stock. What are the "big things" you accomplished in the month just ending? What are the important things for the month ahead? And, yes, you need to do a checkup on finances. This doesn't have to be a big, all-day adventure. Just 30-60 minutes. Give yourself an overview.

Our emotional state varies due to a lot of short-term forces. This include your financial situation, interactions with your family, the drive to work, and the music you last listened to. Keep this in mind. Sometimes we can feel that the month was totally unproductive when, in fact, we knocked off three major projects and came out ten per cent ahead of last year. Acknowledge those wins.

And if you missed your targets and the projects never quite got to completion? Well, acknowledge that as well. Take a minute to look at the bigger picture and determine what you'll do to catch up.

I've created a simple form that you can use at the end of each month to take stock of accomplishments and make notes for the month ahead. It also has a few fields for finances. Don't forget to keep your finger on the financial pulse of your company.

Note: When filling this out, here's an example of how the date format works:

Completed   _____December 27th_____

for the months of   _____December / January___

We have provided three months' worth. In the downloads is a pdf of this form so you can print additional pages.

Monthly Performance Notes

Completed: _____

For the Months of: _____ / _____

Performance for the Month

Projected Income: ___ $ _____   Actual Income: _____ $ _____

Projected Expenses: __ $ _____   Actual Expenses: ____ $ _____

Projected Profit: _____ $ _____   Actual Profit: _ $ _____

Major projects completed internally: _____

_____

_____

Major projects completed for clients: _____

_____

_____

The Month Ahead

Projected Income: ___ $ _____

Projected Expenses: __ $ _____

Projected Profit: _____ $ _____

Major projects we plan to complete: _____

_____

_____

Additional notes: _____

_____

_____

_____

_____

Monthly Performance Notes

Completed: _____

For the Months of: _____ / _____

Performance for the Month

Projected Income: ___$_____   Actual Income: _____$_____

Projected Expenses: _$_____   Actual Expenses: ____$_____

Projected Profit: ____$_____   Actual Profit: _$_____

Major projects completed internally: _____

_____

_____

Major projects completed for clients: _____

_____

_____

The Month Ahead

Projected Income: ___$_____

Projected Expenses: _$_____

Projected Profit: ____$_____

Major projects we plan to complete: _____

_____

_____

Additional notes: _____

_____

_____

_____

_____

_____

Monthly Performance Notes

Completed: _____

For the Months of: _____ / _____

Performance for the Month

Projected Income: ___ $ _____   Actual Income: _____ $ _____

Projected Expenses: _ $ _____   Actual Expenses: ____ $ _____

Projected Profit: ____ $ _____   Actual Profit: _ $ _____

Major projects completed internally: _____

_____

_____

Major projects completed for clients: _____

_____

_____

The Month Ahead

Projected Income: ___ $ _____

Projected Expenses: _ $ _____

Projected Profit: ____ $ _____

Major projects we plan to complete: _____

_____

_____

Additional notes: _____

_____

_____

_____

_____

_____

SMALL BIZ THOUGHTS
TECHNOLOGY COMMUNITY
Training, Resources, & Community for IT Service Providers

Smallbizthoughts.org

Weekly Meetings

Expert Roundtables

Community Forums

White Papers

Audio Programs

SOPs

Checklists

Books

Videos

Webinars

Live Events

Classes

Workbooks

... More!

Stop doing it alone!

Your next prospect needs to know you've got what it takes. Build your processes, hire your next employee, build your business with intention.

All with the Small Biz Thoughts Technology Community.

Monthly Notes

In your monthly sit-down with yourself (or your team), you should take note of things that you would like to do next year. Some of these might be new projects. Others might fall into the category of things to do differently than you did this year.

Each month, as you're making notes for the month, flip to these last pages and makes notes about anything that's future focused: Next year and beyond. Remember, you need to be clear! Don't write a note so cryptic that you won't understand it eight months from now.

I recommend that you try to write in full sentences, or use bullet points that are almost full sentences. "LinkedIn Targeting" is a horrible note. Even if you knew what it meant when you wrote, you certainly won't know the context a year later.

You can include observations about things you did this year, such as evaluating a marketing campaign or client-facing event. You may also make notes about new products and services to review for your solution stack. Any notes that might be helpful to your future self are appropriate.

Notes: _____

_____

_____

_____

_____

_____

_____

_____

_____

_____

_____

Notes: _____

_____

_____

_____

_____

_____

_____

_____

_____

_____

_____

_____

_____

_____

_____

_____

_____

_____

_____

_____

_____

_____

_____

_____

_____

Notes: _____

_____

_____

_____

_____

_____

_____

_____

_____

_____

_____

_____

_____

_____

_____

_____

_____

_____

_____

_____

_____

_____

_____

_____

_____

_____

_____

_____

Notes: _____

_____

_____

_____

_____

_____

_____

_____

_____

_____

_____

_____

_____

_____

_____

_____

_____

_____

_____

_____

_____

_____

_____

_____

_____

_____

_____

Resources: Books to Add to Your List

If there's one habit that has served me well over the years, it's reading. Here are some of my top choices. Note also that many of these are available as audio books.

In the super-connected Internet world, it's important to turn off the screens and focus your mind. Even one hour of reading per day can dramatically improve your business. A wide variety of topics will also seed your brain. Your unconscious mind will start rearranging the ideas you expose yourself to.

Then, when you least expect it, your brain will put together ideas from seemingly-unrelated books. Ultimately, "creativity" consists of combining ideas is new and interesting ways.

So dig in!

Note: Please browse through these and start with titles or authors that appeal to you. There's no reason to read them in alphabetical order by title. Note, also, that there are some very popular books that are not on the list because I found them to be boring or filled with bad advice. Some popular books should have been a blog post. Just sayin.

Actually, the main reason popular books didn't make the list is because I disagree with their philosophy. Two examples are *The Art of War* by Sun Tzu and *The 4-Hour Work Week* by Tim Ferriss. Each of those has a few quotable notes, but neither of them reflects the ethics that I go to market with.

[And I've thrown my books in there just for fun.]

My Top Picks

If I had to force you to read fifteen books, this is where I'd start. (In alpha order by title.)

Awakening the Entrepreneur Within by Michael E. Gerber.

Drive: The Surprising Truth About What Motivates Us by Daniel H. Pink.

Expert Secrets: The Underground Playbook for Converting Your Online Visitors into Lifelong Customers by Russell Brunson.

Factfulness: Ten Reasons We're Wrong About the World - and Why Things Are Better Than You Think by Hans Rosling, Anna Rosling Rönnlund, Ola Rosling.

Great by Choice by Jim Collins, Morten T. Hansen.

Million Dollar Consulting by Alan Weiss.

Relax Focus Succeed by Karl W. Palachuk.

Start with Why: How Great Leaders Inspire Everyone to Take Action by Simon Sinek.

The Absolutely Unbreakable Rules of Service Delivery: How to Manage Your Business to Maximize Customer Service, Profit, and Employee Culture by Karl W. Palachuk.

The Checklist Manifesto: How to Get Things Right by Atul Gawande.

The E-Myth Revisited by Michael E. Gerber.

The Innovator's Solution: Creating and Sustaining Successful Growth by Clayton M. Christensen, Michael E. Raynor.

The Power of Habit: Why We Do What We Do in Life and Business by Charles Duhigg.

The War of Art: Winning the Inner Creative Battle by Steven Pressfield.

Thinking, Fast and Slow by Daniel Kahneman.

Yes, these are repeated below in the big list.

Quotes . . . to prime your reticular Activating System

"Living and Dreaming are two different things–but you can't do one without the other."

— Malcolm Forbes

"Many are stubborn in pursuit of the path they have chosen, few in pursuit of the goal."

— Friedrich Nietzsche

"Men occasionally stumble over the truth, but most of them pick themselves up and hurry off as if nothing had happened."

— Winston Churchill

The Big, Big List of Recommended Books

13 Things Mentally Strong People Don't Do: Take Back Your Power, Embrace Change, Face Your Fears, and Train Your Brain for Happiness and Success by Amy Morin.

30 Days to an Ultra-Positive Attitude by Tommy Newberry.

A Guide to Getting It by Laura Davis, et al.

A Whole New Mind: Why Right-Brainers Will Rule the Future by Daniel H. Pink.

Alone Together: Why We Expect More from Technology and Less from Each Other by Sherry Turkle.

As a Man Thinketh by James Allen.

Atomic Habits: An Easy & Proven Way to Build Good Habits & Break Bad Ones by James Clear.

Awakening the Entrepreneur Within by Michael E. Gerber.

Best Practices in Customer Service by Ron Zemke and John A. Woods.

Better Than Before: Mastering the Habits of Our Everyday Lives by Gretchen Rubin.

Blue Ocean Strategy: How to Create Uncontested Market Space and Make Competition Irrelevant by W. Chan Kim, Renee Mauborgne.

Book Yourself Solid: the Fastest, Easiest, and Most Reliable System for Getting More Clients by Michael Port.

Brand Identity Breakthrough: How to Craft Your Company's Unique Story to Make Your Products Irresistible by Gregory V. Diehl.

Break Through the Noise by Elisa Southard.

Brian Tracy's 21 Secrets to Success by Brian Tracy.

Building Your Business, Leading Your Business, Protecting Your Business by Loral Langemeier (CD set).

Bull's-Eye: The Power of Focus by Brian Tracy.

Business Plan in a Month: Build the Roadmap Your Business Deserves by Karl W. Palachuk.

Business Process Improvement Workbook by H. James Harrington, et al.

Businesses Don't Fail They Commit Suicide: How to Survive Success and Thrive in Good Times and Bad by Larry Mandelberg.

Cloud Services in a Month: Build a Successful Cloud Service Business in 30 Days by Karl W. Palachuk.

Concentration! by Sam Horn and Michael Crisp.

Contagious: Why Things Catch On by Jonah Berger.

Creating A Life Worth Living by Carol Lloyd.

Ctrl Alt Delete: Reboot Your Business. Reboot Your Life. Your Future Depends on It by Mitch Joel.

Customer Service 101 by Renee Evenson.

Daily Readings from Your Best Life Now by Joel Osteen.

Daring Greatly: How the Courage to Be Vulnerable Transforms the Way We Live, Love, Parent, and Lead by Brené Brown PhD.

Dave Ramsey's Complete Guide to Money: The Handbook of Financial Peace University by Dave Ramsey.

Deep Work: Rules for Focused Success in a Distracted World by Cal Newport.

Delivering Happiness: A Path to Profits, Passion, and Purpose by Tony Hsieh.

DotCom Secrets: The Underground Playbook for Growing Your Company Online by Russell Brunson, Dan Kennedy.

Don't Just Do Something, Sit There by Sylvia Boorstein.

Don't Set Goals (The Old Way) by Wade Cook.

Drive: The Surprising Truth About What Motivates Us by Daniel H. Pink.

Emotional Intelligence 2.0 by Travis Bradberry, Jean Greaves.

Emotional Intelligence by Daniel Goleman Ph.D.

E-Myth Mastery by Michael E. Gerber.

Epic Content Marketing: How to Tell a Different Story, Break through the Clutter, and Win More Customers by Marketing Less by Joe Pulizzi.

Execution: The Discipline of Getting Things Done by Larry Bossidy, Ram Charan.

Expert Secrets: The Underground Playbook for Converting Your Online Visitors into Lifelong Customers by Russell Brunson.

Factfulness: Ten Reasons We're Wrong About the World - and Why Things Are Better Than You Think by Hans Rosling, Anna Rosling Rönnlund, Ola Rosling.

Falling Upward: A Spirituality for the Two Halves of Life by Richard Rohr.

Flash Foresight: How to See the Invisible and Do the Impossible by Daniel Burrus, John David Mann.

Flow: Living at the Peak of Your Abilities by Mihaly Csikszentmihalyi Ph.D.

Flow: The Psychology of Optimal Experience by Mihaly Csikszentmihalyi.

Future Cities: 42 Insights and Interviews with Influencers, Startups, Investors by Stefano L. Tresca.

Getting in the Gap by Wayne W. Dyer.

Goal Set Your Way to Achieving Your Dreams by Mark D. Csordos.

Goal Setting 101: How to Set and Achieve A Goal! by Gary Ryan Blair.

God Help Me! This Stress Is Driving Me Crazy by Gregory Popcak.

Good to Great: Why Some Companies Make the Leap...And Others Don't by Jim Collins.

Great by Choice by Jim Collins, Morten T. Hansen.

Grow Something Besides Old by Laurie Beth Jones.

Growing A Business by Paul Hawken.

Habits of the Mind by Archibald Hart.

Happy Yoga by Steve Ross.

How the Body Knows Its Mind: The Surprising Power of the Physical Environment to Influence How You Think and Feel by Sian Beilock.

How to Talk to Anyone: 92 Little Tricks for Big Success in Relationships by Leil Lowndes.

How Now by Raphael Cushnir.

How the Mind Works by Steven Pinker.

I Don't Know: in Praise of Admitting Ignorance and Doubt (Except When You Shouldn't) by Leah Hager Cohen.

Impactful Inclusion Toolkit: 52 Activities to Help You Learn and Practice Inclusion Every Day in the Workplace by Steele, Yvette

In Search of Values by Dr. Sidney B. Simon.

Influence : The Psychology of Persuasion by Robert B. Cialdini.

It's Never Crowded Along the Extra Mile: 10 Secrets for Success and Inner Peace by Dr. Wayne W. Dyer.

Launch: An Internet Millionaire's Secret Formula to Sell Almost Anything Online, Build a Business You Love, and Live the Life of Your Dreams by Jeff Walker.

Leaders Eat Last: Why Some Teams Pull together and Others Don't by Simon Sinek.

Leadership Essentials for Successful Executives by James Kernan.

Learn to Relax by Mike George.

Life Is an Attitude by Elwood N. Chapman.

Living Your Best Life by Laura Berman.

Making Good Habits, Breaking Bad Habits: 14 New Behaviors That Will Energize Your Life by Joyce Meyer.

Making Peace with Your Past by H. Norman Wright.

Making Work Visible: Exposing Time Theft to Optimize Work & Flow by Dominica Degrandis.

Managed Services in a Month: Build a Successful, Modern Computer Consulting Business in 30 Days, 3rd Edition by Karl W. Palachuk.

Managed Services Operations Manual (4 vol set) by Karl W. Palachuk.

Managing for Results by Peter Drucker.

Mastering the Rockefeller Habits: What You Must Do to increase the Value of Your Growing Firm by Verne Harnish.

Maximum Success by James Waldroop Ph.D., Timothy Butler Ph.D.

Million Dollar Consulting by Alan Weiss.

Mindset: The New Psychology of Success by Carol Dweck.

Never Split the Difference: Negotiating as if Your Life Depended on It by Chris Voss.

Noise: A Flaw in Human Judgment by Daniel Kahneman, Olivier Sibony, Cass R. Sunstein.

Open Mind, Open Heart by Thomas Keating.

Outliers: The Story of Success by Malcolm Gladwell.

Package, Price, Profit: The Essential Guide to Packaging and Pricing Your MSP Plans by Nigel Moore.

Perfecting Ourselves by Aaron Hoopes.

Permission Marketing by Seth Godin.

Play Bigger: How Pirates, Dreamers, and innovators Create and Dominate Markets by Al Ramadan, Dave Peterson, Christopher Lochhead, Kevin Maney.

Power Vs. Force by David R. Hawkins.

Predictably Irrational: The Hidden Forces That Shape Our Decisions by Dan Ariely.

Process and the other 'P' Word (Which is also Process) by Allen Edwards.
https://www.amazon.com/Process-Other-Word-Which-Also/dp/B0BGNCJYM3

Profit First: Transform Your Business from a Cash-Eating Monster to a Money-Making Machine by Mike Michalowicz.

Project Management in Small Business - How to Deliver Successful, Profitable Projects on Time with Your Small Business Clients by Dana J Goulston and Karl W. Palachuk.

Purple Cow by Seth Godin.

Putting the One Minute Manager to Work by Kenneth Blanchard and Robert Lorber.

Quote Me On This: The Wit and Wisdom of Coleman Cox by Coleman Cox and Karl W. Palachuk.

Raving Fans by Ken Blanchard and Sheldon Bowles.

Real Magic by Wayne Dyer.

Reclaiming Conversation: The Power of Talk in a Digital Age by Sherry Turkle.

Reengineering Yourself: Using Tomorrow's Success Tools to Excel Today by Dan Burrus.

Relax Focus Succeed by Karl W. Palachuk.

Rhythms of Life by William Bailley.

Rising Strong: How the Ability to Reset Transforms the Way We Live, Love, Parent, and Lead by Brené Brown.

Secrets of Question-Based Selling: How the Most Powerful Tool in Business Can Double Your Sales Results by Thomas A. Freese.

Self-Directed Behavior: Self-Modification for Personal Adjustment by David L. Watson, Roland G. Tharp.

Service Agreements for SMB Consultants - Revised Edition: A Quick-Start Guide to Managed Services by Karl W. Palachuk.

Silence & Stillness in Every Season by John Main, et al.

Six Pixels of Separation: Everyone Is Connected. Connect Your Business to Everyone by Mitch Joel.

So Good they Can't Ignore You: Why Skills Trump Passion in the Quest for Work You Love by Cal Newport.

Soonish: Ten Emerging Technologies That'll Improve and/or Ruin Everything by Kelly Weinersmith, Zach Weinersmith.

Start with Why: How Great Leaders Inspire Everyone to Take Action by Simon Sinek.

Stop Whining and Start Winning by Frank Pacetta, Roger Gittines.

Strategic Planning for Success by Roger Kaufman, et al.

Subtract: The Untapped Science of Less by Leidy Klotz.

Success Rate Marketing: How Small Businesses Can Leverage KPIs and Stop Losing Money by Brandon Doyle.

Success Through A Positive Mental Attitude by W. Clement Stone.

Successes That Happened Without Any Effort by Karl W. Palachuk.

Super Service by Jeff Gee, Val Gee.

Take Time for Your Life by Cheryl Richardson.

The 10X Rule: The Only Difference Between Success and Failure by Grant Cardone.

The 22 Immutable Laws of Marketing by Al Ries.

The 4 Disciplines of Execution: Achieving Your Wildly Important Goals by Sean Covey, Chris McChesney, Jim Huling.

The 8th Habit: from Effectiveness to Greatness by Stephen R. Covey.

The Absolutely Unbreakable Rules of Service Delivery: How to Manage Your Business to Maximize Customer Service, Profit, and Employee Culture by Karl W. Palachuk.

The Anticipatory Organization: Turn Disruption and Change into Opportunity and Advantage by Daniel Burrus.

The Big Leap by Gay Hendricks.

The Buckets of Money Retirement Solution: The Ultimate Guide to Income for Life by Raymond J. Lucia.

The Checklist Manifesto: How to Get Things Right by Atul Gawande.

The Compassionate Geek: How Engineers, IT Pros, and Other Tech Specialists Can Master Human Relations Skills to Deliver Outstanding Customer Service by Don Crawley.

The Culture Map: Breaking Through the invisible Boundaries of Global Business by Erin Meyer.

The E-Myth Contractor by Michael Gerber.

The E-Myth Manager by Michael Gerber.

The E-Myth Revisited by Michael E. Gerber.

The Essential Drucker: in One Volume the Best of Sixty Years of Peter Drucker's Essential Writings on Management by Peter F. Drucker.

The Experience Economy, with a New Preface by the Authors: Competing for Customer Time, Attention, and Money by B. Joseph Pine II, James H. Gilmore.

The Five Dysfunctions of a Team: A Leadership Fable by Patrick Lencioni.

The Five Laws That Determine All of Life's Outcomes by Brett Harward.

The Four: The Hidden DNA of Amazon, Apple, Facebook, and Google by Scott Galloway.

The Geography of Genius: A Search for the World's Most Creative Places from Ancient Athens to Silicon Valley by Eric Weiner.

The Habit Fix: The New Habit Guide to Getting Happy and Healthy in 7 Simple Steps by Eileen Rose Giadone.

The Importance of Being Lazy by Al Gini.

The Inevitable: Understanding the 12 Technological Forces That Will Shape Our Future by Kevin Kelly.

The Innovator's Dilemma: When New Technologies Cause Great Firms to Fail by Clayton M. Christensen.

The Innovator's Solution: Creating and Sustaining Successful Growth by Clayton M. Christensen, Michael E. Raynor.

The Innovators: How a Group of Hackers, Geniuses, and Geeks Created the Digital Revolution by Walter Isaacson.

The IT Business Owner's Survival Guide: How to Save Time, Avoid Stress and Build a Successful IT Business by Richard Tubb.

The Little Red Book of Selling by Jeffrey Gitomer.

The Long Tail: Why the Future of Business Is Selling Less of More by Chris Anderson.

The Magic Lamp by Keith Ellis.

The Network Migration Workbook: Zero Downtime Migration Strategies for Windows Networks 2nd Edition by Karl W. Palachuk, Manuel L. Palachuk.

The New Economics, Third Edition: for industry, Government, Education by W. Edwards Deming.

The Nonfiction Book Publishing Plan: The Professional Guide to Profitable Self-Publishing by Stephanie Chandler and Karl W. Palachuk.

The Obstacle Is the Way: The Timeless Art of Turning Trials into Triumph by Ryan Holiday.

The One Minute Manager by Kenneth Blanchard and Spencer Johnson.

The Paradox of Choice: Why More is Less by Barry Schwartz.

The Path by Laurie Beth Jones.

The Power of Clarity by Brian Tracy.

The Power of Habit: Why We Do What We Do in Life and Business by Charles Duhigg.

The Power of Vulnerability: Teachings of Authenticity, Connection, and Courage by Brené Brown.

The Psychology of Achievement by Brian Tracy.

The Relaxation & Stress Reduction Workbook by Martha Davis, Matthew, Ph.D. McKay, Elizabeth Robbins Eshelman.

The Small Biz Quickstart Workbook: The Ultimate Guide for First-Time Entrepreneurs by Karl W. Palachuk.

The Speed of Trust: The One Thing that Changes Everything by Stephen M. R. Covey.

The Spirit of Leadership by Fr. Robert J. Spitzer.

The Thirty-Six Strategies of Ancient China by Stefan Verstappen.

The Tipping Point: How Little Things Can Make a Big Difference by Malcolm Gladwell.

The Ultimate Gift by Jim Stovall.

The War of Art: Winning the Inner Creative Battle by Steven Pressfield.

Thinking, Fast and Slow by Daniel Kahneman.

Uncommon Service: How to Win by Putting Customers at the Core of Your Business by Frances Frei, Anne Morriss.

The Walk-On Method to Career & Business Success: 31 Underdogs Who Became Extraordinary (And So Can You!) by Jim Roddy.

The Way You Do Anything is the Way You Do Everything: The Why of Why Your Business Isn't Making More Money by Suzanne Evans.

To Sell Is Human: The Surprising Truth about Moving Others by Daniel H. Pink.

Traction: Get a Grip on Your Business by Gino Wickman.

Transform Your Business by Being Remarkable.

Twelve Ways to Develop A Positive Attitude by Dale E. Galloway.

UnMarketing: Stop Marketing. Start Engaging by Scott Stratten, Alison Kramer.

What Are Your Goals by Gary Ryan Blair.

What Do You Really Want? How to Set A Goal and Go for It! by Beverly K. Bachel.

What the Most Successful People Do Before Breakfast: A Short Guide to Making Over Your Mornings--and Life by Laura Vanderkam.

Why Did the Chicken Cross the World?: The Epic Saga of the Bird That Powers Civilization by Andrew Lawler.

Why Not? by Barry J. Nalebuff, Ian Ayres.

Women of Color in Tech: A Blueprint for Inspiring and Mentoring the Next Generation of Technology Innovators by Susanne Tedrick.

You: The Owner's Manual by Michael F. Roizen et al.

You, Inc.: The Art of Selling Yourself by Harry Beckwith, Christine Clifford Beckwith.

Your Best Life Now by Joel Osteen.

Your Best Year Ever: A 5-Step Plan for Achieving Your Most Important Goals by Michael Hyatt.

HUGE Thank You

. . . To The ASCII Group and Gozynta

For helping bring this book to you.

Great partners make great things possible.

Check them out at www.ASCII.com and www.Gozynta.com.

Quotes . . . to prime your reticular Activating System

"Most barriers to success are man-made. And most often, you're the man who made them."

— Frank Tyger

"No man ever made a great discovery without the exercise of the imagination."

— George Henry Lewes

"Nothing can stop the man with the right mental attitude from achieving his goal; nothing on earth can help the man with the wrong mental attitude."

— W.W. Ziege

Resources: Blogs, Web Sites, Newsletters, and Podcasts to Explore

Web Sites

- The ASCII Group – www.ascii.com

- Bigger Brains www.GetBiggerBrains.com

- Bigger Brains MSP website www.BiggerMSP.com

- The Business of Tech Podcast (Dave Sobel) – http://businessof.tech/

- ChannelPro SMB – Channelpronetwork.com

- Cheeky Sales Coach – Cheekysalescoach.com

- Howard M. Cohen - http://www.howardmcohen.com

- Howard M. Cohen's Substack is at Business Technologist's Journal

- Robert D. Crane – http://www.ciaops.com

- Gozynta - tools for MSPs – https://www.gozynta.com

- Paul Green – https://www.paulgreensmspmarketing.com/

- Growably – https://growably.com

- IT Service Provider University – ITSPU.com – Classes from Small Biz Thoughts

- James Kernan – Kernanconsulting.com

- Karl's Store – Store.smallbizthoughts.com

- M365 maps – https://www.m365maps.com

- MSP Business Evaluation Tool – https://eurekaprocess.com/msp-business-evaluation/

- National Society of IT Service Providers – nsitsp.org

- Manuel Palachuk – Manuelpalachuk.com

- Relax Focus Succeed – Relaxfocussucceed.com

- Erick Simpson – Ericksimpson.com

- Small Biz Thoughts – Smallbizthoughts.com / Smallbizthoughts.org

- SMB TechFest – SMBTechFest.com

- The Tech Tribe – https://thetechtribe.com

- Third Tier / Amy Babinchak – https://www.thirdtier.net

- Richard Tubb's Newsletter – Tubblog.co.uk/nl (Newsletter)

- Richard Tubb Stuff – https://www.tubblog.co.uk/

Blogs

- Amy Babinchak – https://www.thirdtier.net

- Robert Crane – Blog.ciaops.com

- Karl's blog – Blog.smallbizthoughts.com

- Howard M. Cohen blogs at https://rcpmag.com/blogs/the-evolving-msp/list/blog-list.aspx
  and https://adtmag.com/articles/list/the-citizen-developer.aspx

- Robert D. Crane – Blog - http://blog.ciaops.com

- Paul Green – https://www.paulgreensmspmarketing.com/learning-hub/

- National Society of IT Service Providers – nsitsp.org/news

- Karl Palachuk's Relax Focus Succeed – Relaxfocussucceed.com/blog

- Manuel Palachuk – Manuelpalachuk.com

- Richard Tubb – https://www.tubblog.co.uk/blog/

Podcasts

- Eric Anthony – https://itunes.apple.com/WebObjects/MZStore.woa/wa/viewPodcast?id=1679331639

- The Business of Tech Podcast (Dave Sobel)
  Apple Podcasts: https://link.chtbl.com/LfTLq2dJ

- Cheeky Sales Coach (by Karl W. Palachuk) www.cheekysalescoach.com

- Robert D. Crane Podcast – http://ciaops.podbean.com

- Paul Green – https://www.paulgreensmspmarketing.com/podcast-intro/

- IT Business Podcast – https://www.itbusinesspodcast.com/

- The Killing IT Podcast – KillingIT.smallbizthoughts.com

- PSA Impact (Chris Timm and Rayanne Buchianico) – https://psaimpact.net/podcasts/
- SMB Community Podcast – SMBcommunitypodcast.com
- Richard Tubb – https://tubb.co/tubbtalk

Video Channels

- All Things MSP – https://youtube.com/@AllThingsMSP
- Bigger Brains – https://www.youtube.com/@BiggerBrains1
- Business of Tech with Dave Sobel – https://www.youtube.com/mspradio
- Robert D. Crane channel – http://www.youtube.com/@directorcia
- Eureka Process - Videos for MSP Growth on YouTube – https://www.youtube.com/@EurekaProcess
- Paul Green – https://www.youtube.com/mspmarketing
- IT Business Podcast – https://www.youtube.com/c/ITBusinessPodcast
- James Kernan – https://youtube.com/@VARCOACH
- Lawrence Systems – Youtube.com/channel/UCHkYOD-3fZbuGhwsADBd9ZQ
- MSP Radio – Youtube.com/channel/UCu0s5jO5LM-iLZgOK_seAzA
- National Society of IT Service Providers – youtube.com/nsitsp
- Relax Focus Succeed – Youtube.com/channel/UCJO-Llw44FQFoqTjjrgv46Q
- Robin Robins – Youtube.com/channel/UCR9dQAmN23rvTuVQeMBIDGw
- Rocket MSP – Youtube.com/channel/UCLtROkrTxzaTx-4ywE5m4mQ
- Small Biz Thoughts – Youtube.com/smallbizthoughts
- SMB Nation – Youtube.com/channel/UC_bHCHs8vkT9pVB-vVz-vFg
- The Tech Tribe – https://www.youtube.com/thetechtribe
- Richard Tubb – https://www.youtube.com/@Tubblog_MSP

Social Media Pages and Groups

- All Things MSP – Facebook Group – https://www.facebook.com/groups/allthingsmsp/
- All Things MSP – LinkedIn Page – https://www.linkedin.com/company/allthingsmsp/

- IT Business Podcast – https://www.facebook.com/itbusinesspodcast

- IT Documentation Users Group – https://www.facebook.com/groups/ITDUG/

- Ransomware and Security https://www.facebook.com/groups/RansomwarePrevention

- Intune, Lighthouse and Defender https://www.facebook.com/groups/endpointmanager

- Legislation and Regulation
  https://www.facebook.com/groups/MSPRegulationAndLegislation

- National Society of IT Service Providers Facebook Page:
  https://www.facebook.com/National-Society-of-I-T-Service-Providers-108845781574908

- National Society of IT Service Providers LinkedIn Page:
  https://www.linkedin.com/company/national-society-of-it-service-providers/

On-Demand Classes

- All the stuff at **Bigger Brains** - https://getbiggerbrains.com

- **Robert D. Crane** online training – https://www.ciaopsacademy.com

- All the stuff at **IT Service Provider University** – https://www.itspu.com

  o Absolutely Unbreakable Rules of Service Delivery

  o Automate Your QuickBooks Online Accounting

  o Business Strategy Made Easy

  o Cloud Services in a Month: Applying the Book

  o Core Standard Operating Procedures for SMB ITs

  o Creating a Great Lead Generation Program

  o Customer Service for IT Service Providers

  o Deep Dive Into Facebook, YouTube and LinkedIn

  o Financial Processes for the IT Services Firm

  o Highly Successful Project Management

  o Introduction to Relax Focus Succeed

  o Leadership and Management Principles for MSPs

  o Making the Most of QuickBooks Desktop in an IT Service Business

  o Managed Services in a Month – Applying the Book

- o Managing Your Service Board

- o MSP Professional Sales Program

- o Optimize Your Social Media Marketing

- o Position Your IT Firm for Growth or Sale

- o Powerhouse of One: How To Be A Super Successful Solo MSP

- o Profit First for MSPs

- o Service Agreements for SMB Consultants

- o Supercharge Your Social Media

- o Surviving the Success of Your Growing Business

- o The Most Important Checklists for Any IT Service Provider

- o The Unbreakable Rules of PSA

- All the stuff in the **Small Biz Thoughts Technology Community**:
  www.smallbizthoughts.org

  - o A Practical Introduction to Relax Focus Succeed

  - o Build a Client Newsletter that Works

  - o Building the Basic Small Business Network

  - o Client Onboarding for Managed Services

  - o Deep Dive into the Client Roadmap Process

  - o DNS Training - What You Ned to Know

  - o Employee Onboarding

  - o Finding and Keeping Great Employees

  - o How to Get New Clients - Especially if You're Starting Out or Starting Over

  - o Key Performance Indicators for IT Service Managers

  - o Move Yourself and Your Clients to Managed Service

  - o Social Media Super Charge

  - o Supercharge Hiring, Team Building, and Sales with DISC

  - o TCP/IP Troubleshooting

- o Tune Up Your YouTube Channel
- o Weeding Your Client Garden
- o Year of Intention

Live Classes

- See the current live classes at IT Service Provider University – https://www.itspu.com
- See the current live classes in the Small Biz Thoughts Technology Community: https://www.smallbizthoughts.org

---

A Few Final Resources

Karl's Weekly Newsletter – The Small Biz Thoughts newsletter has been providing news and commentary (and sometimes fun) to the SMB IT consulting community for almost twenty years. With 10,000 subscribers and an insanely high open rate, it is one of the most-read resources for IT consultants of all kinds.

Visit **https://smallbizthoughts.com/newsletter/**

Our Store – The Small Biz Thoughts store is a place where you can find a handful of free goodies, plus all of Karl's books in all formats. Plus there's some other fun stuff there. Note: If you join the Small Biz Thoughts Technology Community, you get pretty much all of it included. But if you want the hard-copy version, it's in the store.

Visit **https://store.smallbizthoughts.com**

IT Service Provider University – Our training center. Now with more than twenty-five 5-week courses covering everything from finances to business strategy, the managed service business model, and running your IT service department. All classes include lots of hand-outs, practical application advice, and even office hours with the instructor. Plus, we have a certification program.

Visit **https://itspu.com**

Prime Questions

As promised way back at the beginning of this workbook, this section simply gathers up the Prime Questions from throughout the rest of the workbook. You may find these useful to help yourself or you staff start getting in the right mindset thinking about your business.

Prime Questions from: Priming Your Brain

1. How has your business been going so far this year?

_____

2. Is there anything that troubles you about your business now or in the months ahead? If so, what?

_____

3. Who are your favorite clients?

_____

4. Do you have the talent (your own or your employees) you need to be successful in the year ahead?

_____

5. What do you like MOST about your business? Do you get enough of it?

_____

Prime Questions from: Report on This Year

1. Did you start this year with a budget and a plan? If so, how are you doing?

_____

_____

2. What's the biggest challenge you have today, and looking through the end of the year?

_____

Small Biz Thoughts Technology Community

3. How much do you like your current mix of productions and services, given current pricing?

_____

_____

Prime Questions from: Company Goals for the Next Year

1. Are you looking forward to next year with hope, concern, or some mixture of these? Why so?

_____

_____

2. Are you planning any big changes in your business for next year? (This might be with regard to clients, your service offering, employees, or whatever else.)

_____

_____

3. In the big-big picture, will your business be essentially the same next your, or will something important change?

_____

_____

Prime Questions from: Conference Goals Next Year

1. When you attend conferences, where do you find the most value? (e.g., networking, meeting vendors, travel)

_____

_____

2. Which kind of conferences do you get the most value from?

_____

_____

3. After a conference, what do you do to "process" what you learned and the contacts you made?

_____

_____

Prime Questions from: Webinar Goals for Next Year

1. As a rule, how useful have you found webinars in the last year? Why?

_____

_____

2. Is there a general brand or kind of webinar that you find the most useful? What is it, and why is this group of webinars better than others?

_____

_____

3. Over the past year, would you say that you attended too many, too few, or just the right number of webinars or online events?

_____

_____

Prime Questions from: Monthly Tune-Ups

1. Do you ever have the nagging feeling that you're "forgetting something" when it comes to all the details involved in supporting all of your clients? Explain.

_____

_____

2. Does anyone in your company have the job of constantly fine-tuning your operations or improving your finances? If not you, who is this?

_____

_____

3. Do you have a standardized monthly maintenance that is performed at all clients? Is it customized per client?

_____

_____

Prime Questions from: Embrace Outsourcing from Now On

1. How much have you relied on outsourced resources for your business? Will this change in the year ahead?

_____

_____

2. As a rule do you consider outsourced resources to be lower-quality or higher-quality than the talent you have in-house?

_____

_____

3. How open are you to expanding the capabilities of your company by relying on contractors or outsourced personnel?

_____

_____

Prime Questions from: Business Cards at Conferences

1. Do you intentionally take business cards to conferences, or show up without them? Why?

_____

_____

2. Do your consider your business cards to be a marketing resource, a necessary (evil) expense, or something in the middle?

_____

_____

3. Do you collect business cards when you go to meetings? If so, do you actually do anything with them?

_____

_____

Prime Questions from: Monthly Financial Kick in the Butt

1. What is your relationship with money? Do you feel bad or greedy when you focus on money?

_____

_____

2. How often do you review "the big picture" of your business finances?

_____

_____

3. Did you have financial surprises in the last year that you did not anticipate (whether good or bad)?

_____

_____

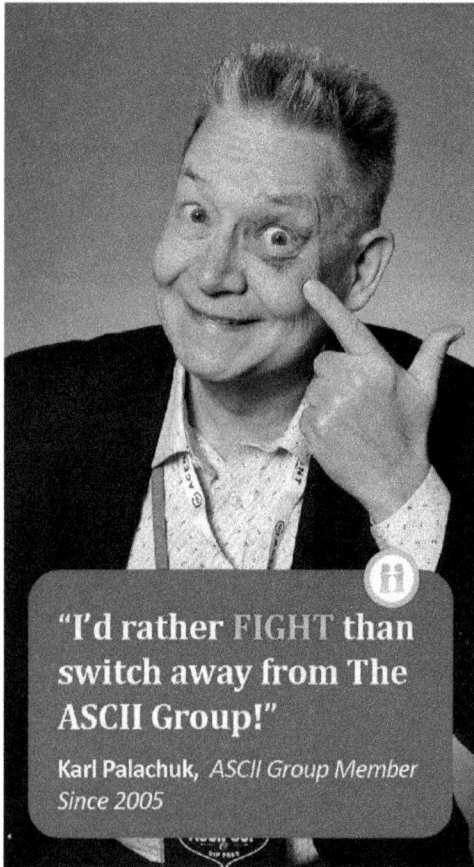

www.ingramcontent.com/pod-product-compliance
Lightning Source LLC
Chambersburg PA
CBHW051756200326

41597CB00025B/4572